IRISH MIS
from the Golden Ag

D0549237

Clonfert Abbey

MARIAN KEANEY

IRISH MISSIONARIES

from the Golden Age to the 20th Century

VERITAS PUBLICATIONS DUBLIN

First published 1985 by
Veritas Publications
7-8 Lower Abbey Street
Dublin 1

ISBN: 0 86217 170 9

Cover design by Angela Young
Illustrated by Kevin O'Brien
Photograph on p. 54 courtesy of the
National Gallery of Ireland; photograph
on p. 75 courtesy of Bord Fáilte

Typesetting by Printset & Design Ltd., Dublin
Printed in the Republic of Ireland by Genprint Ltd, Dublin

Contents

		Page
Foreword		5
1. St Columbanus and his Companions		7
2. St Brendan the Navigator		15
3. St Colmcille		26
4. St Malachy Ó Morgair		40
5. St Oliver Plunkett		48
6. Ypres to Kylemore —		
The Story of the Irish Benedictine Nuns		62
Bibliography		77

For
Teresa, Una, Vincent and Ursula

FOREWORD

The extent of Irish missionary achievement from the sixth century to the present day is truly a phenomenon. During the Golden Age of Irish Christianity this influence was mainly felt on the continent of Europe. However, during the twentieth century it spread to Africa, Asia and South America. These Irish travellers spread not only Christianity, but culture and scholarship as well.

The early missionaries were scribes, sailors and scholars. Later they were reformers, diplomats and builders. The role of the martyred archbishop, St Oliver Plunkett, in promoting Christianity during Penal days in Ireland recently received the official approval of the Catholic Church when he was canonised. The international peace-keeping role of Irish missionaries in recent times has yet to be the subject of a full study. It is regrettable that while the role of combatants down through the centuries has received enormous documentation and media coverage, that of the peace-keepers, those who healed the wounds and built up the new societies has never received adequate acclaim. This book and its predecessor, *They Brought the Good News* (Veritas, 1980) seek to highlight the work of Irish Missionaries through the centuries. Their unique role in the spread of culture, education and medical facilities as well as Christianity is a most neglected aspect of our history which needs further research and study.

I am most grateful to the following for their help and encouragement during the writing of this book. Most Rev Dr Michael Smith, Auxiliary Bishop of Meath; the Benedictines of Kylemore, particularly Sr M Benedict; the staff of Longford-Westmeath library; Marie Bray and Mary Heery for their painstaking typing of the manuscript.

Marian Keaney
Mullingar, December 1984

5

1

ST COLUMBANUS AND HIS COMPANIONS

St Columbanus is the best-known of those Irish missionaries who spread monasticism and culture on the continent of Europe. Even though he founded the great abbey of Bobbio only one year before his death, it is the subject of an enormous amount of literature and research. To this day, there are many churches and shrines dedicated to St Columbanus throughout Italy.

After the death of St Columbanus, his monks adopted the rule of St Benedict, and many recruits for the Benedictine Order came from the monastery of Bobbio. The feast day of St Columban was celebrated as a civil and ecclesiastical holiday in the province of Liguria until 1375 at least. A beautiful little Romanesque church of St Columban was built in the eleventh or twelfth century at Vaprio d'Adda in the diocese of Milan. This church is of considerable importance in the history of sacred art. It is built throughout of hewn stone, and the sculptures in the porch are decorated with fleurs-de-lis. There are four paintings of the Saint in this church, the most interesting of which is painted on wood on the triptych above the altar.

The crypt in the Basilica of St Columbanus at Bobbio was completely renovated in 1910 at the wish of Cardinal Logue, Archbishop of Armagh, and with the help of subscriptions from Ireland. The Saint's body was laid in a beautiful fifteenth-century sarcophagus designed by Giovanni dei Patriarchi, and was placed, together with the remains of many of his successors and disciples, under the new marble altar.

St Francis of Assisi came to Bobbio to visit the tomb of St Columbanus. Biographers of St Francis have told us that there were many similarities between the dress and observances of Francis and Columbanus. The Irish monks wore a tunic of

7

undyed wool with a cowl. The early Franciscan dwellings, little wattled huts with a hedge around them, resembled the early Irish monasteries. The Irish monks generally carried a stout walking stick, a leather water-bottle slung across the shoulder, a wallet containing a few precious books, and some relics of the saints.

St Columbanus was born in the province of Leinster in the middle of the sixth century. He is said to have been well-educated in the classics. At an early age he wrote a commentary on the Psalms and a collection of Latin poems which show that he had considerable skill in the art of versification. He attended the school of the Abbot Sinchell at Killeigh in County Offaly. Then he went to Bangor in County Down where he was taught for some years by St Comgall. Columbanus was ordained a priest in 572, after which he devoted a number of years to literary and sacred studies. He then decided to leave Ireland and visit the Continent.

Although Christianity had been established in France for a long time, constant wars and strife had resulted in the decline of the faith. According to Jonas the historian, 'either from the constant incursions of foreign enemies, or from the neglect and carelessness of the bishops, the power of religion became almost extinct, and nothing but the profession of Christianity remained'.

We do not know if Columbanus was aware of the state of Christianity in France before he left Bangor. Comgall was unhappy when he first heard of his decision, but he eventually consented to his departure. As an indication of his great support for Columbanus' project, he selected twelve companions from Bangor to travel with him, among them St Gall and St Deicholus, both of whom became famous for their missionary work in France and Switzerland.

Columbanus and his companions travelled through England and arrived in France around 590. They then went to Burgundy and the Vosges district, now famous for its vineyards, but then a wild and uncultivated tract of country. There they founded their first settlement. For nine days their only food was the bark of trees, roots, or whatever wild berries they could find in the forests, and they nearly died of starvation.

Chapelle Fontaine de St Columban

In Burgundy Columbanus and his followers founded the monasteries of Annegray, Luxeuil and Fontaines. Luxeuil was the most important of these foundations and its rule was widely adopted by other monasteries throughout France, or Gaul, as the country was then called. In the middle of the seventh century many Gaulish monasteries adopted the rules of Columbanus and Benedict.

As in the great Irish monastic seats of learning, sacred studies, liberal studies, poetry and history were taught at the monasteries of Columbanus. Beautiful handwriting and the art of illumination were used to multiply and adorn copies of the gospels and the works of early Christian writers.

In 610 the monks were expelled from Burgundy by Brunhilda, the ruler of the area. Columbanus was not deterred by this and resumed his wanderings, visiting noble families in order to make their acquaintance and gain their support. It is said that the Irish method of calculating the date of Easter, a subject of controversy among Christian churchmen for years, may have been responsible for the expulsion of Columbanus. He was greatly distressed by the Easter controversy, and wrote in strong terms about it to Pope Gregory the Great. He also sent a letter to the bishops of Gaul. He explained to them that he wished to be allowed to continue his work in France without fear of expulsion from any area, until the Easter controversy was resolved. However, he also argued that the Irish method of calculation was the correct one, since the old Irish were the 'most able Philosophers and Calculators of mathematical tables'. Despite this, he conceded 'that whatever system accords most with the Old and New Testaments should be observed without any ill feeling on the part of anyone'.

This long letter may have helped reconcile Columbanus and the French bishops. However, he and his companions were soon banished for another reason. Columbanus reproved Theodric, a member of the ruling family of Burgundy, for his immoral behaviour. Because of this he was expelled from Burgundy and ordered to return to Ireland. With a few companions he journeyed to Nantes, hoping to set sail for Ireland. As soon as the group boarded the ship, a violent storm blew up, and they could not put out to sea. The ship lay stranded for three days at the mouth of the river and, in exasperation, the captain ordered Columbanus and his friends to disembark. It is said that the storm then abated and the ship set sail, leaving Columbanus and his party behind.

When he left Nantes, Columbanus took refuge with Clotaire II, King of Soissons, who received him very hospitably. He and his followers founded many more monasteries — Faremoutiers in 627, Jouarre in 630, and Rebais in 636. These three monasteries were situated in the Brie area, now famous for its cheese and dairy products. The monastery at Rebais become a favourite resting place for Irish pilgrims journeying to and from Rome. Two of Columbanus' companions settled permanently in Gaul — St Kilian at Aubiguy, and St Fiacra in a hermitage which later grew into the famous monastery at Breuil.

Having stayed at Soissons for some time, Columbanus requested King Clotaire to secure a safe passage for him through the realm of Theodebert, brother of Theodric of Burgundy. However, Theodebert welcomed Columbanus graciously, and we are told that he asked him to remain in his territory, promising 'to find him out lovely places in every way suited to the purposes of servants of God, and neighbouring nations to preach to, within reach on every side'.

Columbanus accepted Theodebert's offer, and based himself in his domain for some time. He and his companions wandered along the Rhine and into Switzerland. He lived for a while at Bregentz on Lake Constance, where he talked to many people who had fallen away from the practice of Christianity. One of his companions, St Gall, became ill with an attack of fever, and, unable to continue the journey, asked Columbanus' permission to remain behind. Gall had already learned the dialect of the area, and had had considerable success in leading the people away from the practice of idolatry. He built a cell near Lake Constance, and had so great an influence in the area that a church was built there in his honour after his death. St Gall was accepted as the apostle of the Swiss nation, and the town and canton of St Gall derive their name from him.

At this time a war broke out in Switzerland and Columbanus wisely decided to cross the Alps into Italy. He was well received in Milan by King Agiluf of Lombardy who granted him a wild stretch of land, the site of a ruined church once dedicated to St Peter. In 614 Columbanus began to build his celebrated monastery of Bobbio on this site. It was to become one of the most famous monastic foundations on the continent of Europe. But Columbanus did not live to see the result of his labours in Italy. He died at Bobbio on 21 November 615 at the age of seventy-two, and his remains rest in the modern church there. In recognition of his work in the area, the beautiful town of San

11

Columbano was named in his memory.

Although Columbanus had a very active career, other aspects of his life also caused his name to be revered. The austerity of the rule of Columbanus was unequalled even by the rule of the early Egyptian hermits. His was probably based on the rule of Bangor, the only surviving rule of Irish origin, written in Latin.

Referring to the rule of Columbanus, Dr James Kenney, in his *Sources for the Early History of Ireland*, says that 'Columbanus gave an extraordinary impetus and a special direction to the growth of monasticism. The rule of Columbanus was widely accepted and long retained even in many monasteries where the rule of St Benedict was adopted by its side'.

A friend of Columbanus, the monk Jonas of Bobbio, wrote a *Life of Columban* which is the source of much valuable information about the man himself, his travels and his monastic foundations. Jonas tells us that when Columbanus arrived at Luxeuil, he found it ruined by the ravages of Attila the Hun. Not only the town, but the crops too, had been destroyed by the barbarians, and after some time a vast stretch of countryside around Burgundy became covered by forests inhabited almost solely by wild animals. Some miles from Luxeuil, near the wood of Jupiter, there were ruins of a Gaulish temple to the goddess Diana. According to Jonas, it was on the site of this temple that Columbanus and his companions first established themsleves until he founded his first permanent monastery at Luxeuil.

In his wanderings through the mountains Columbanus found a wolf's lair. He drove the wolf away and often retired to this secluded place to pray. The cave is overshadowed by a great mass of rock, and surrounded by trees. A spring, known as the Holy Well of St Columban, flows from the rock at the side of the cave. According to the legends of the area, squirrels and doves played in the folds of his cowl, the birds nestled in his palms and the wild beasts obeyed his commands. It is said that a bear abandoned the carcass of a stag when Columbanus told him that his monks wanted the animal's hide to make shoes for themselves.

There are now almost no traces of details of the original building of the monastery at Luxeuil where nobles brought their sons to be educated. It is possible that the monks followed the

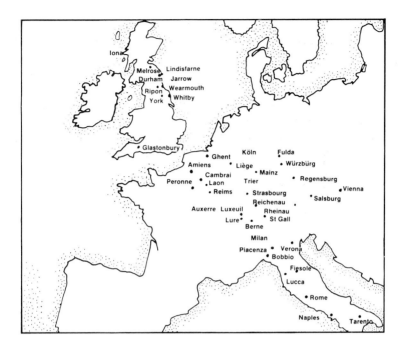

Irish Monastic Foundations in Britain and Europe

Irish custom of erecting a number of huts in groups around an oratory. Clothair II took the monastery under his protection and enriched it with gifts. In the centuries that followed the monastery was attacked by barbarian tribes and destroyed.

The layout of the monastery of Annegrai is said to have resembled some of the early Irish foundations such as Glendalough. It was built of unhewn stone and was so famous that within two or three years of its foundation about 600 monks had assembled there. These later moved to Luxeuil.

Fontaines, the third monastery founded by St Columbanus, was also situated in a beautiful forest. Columbanus and his followers drained the marshes and cultivated the land. The present priory of Fontaines houses stained-glass windows which depict Columbanus holding the plan of the church and draining the marshes. There is a painting of the Saint in a chapel at the

13

north side of the altar. He is holding a scroll which reads 'He sought a place and built another monastery, which he named Fontaines'.

In the year 600 St Columbanus and the Irish monks were expelled from Luxeuil. One old monk, St Deicola, was too old and infirm to continue the long journey on foot, so he decided to remain behind in the forest. He put his tent up beside a well, and soon afterwards was visited by King Clothair II who was hunting boar in the forest. When Deicola told him who he was, the King gave him a grant of the forests, pastures and fisheries in the neighbourhood and a town named Bredena.

2

ST BRENDAN THE NAVIGATOR

The legendary voyages of St Brendan have been the subject of much lore and discussion. Geographical scholars are still debating whether or not the so-called Hy-Breasil which Brendan sought was in fact part of the United States. There is considerable evidence to support the theory that Brendan and his fellow sailors set foot in America more than 900 years before Columbus arrived there in 1492. The primary sources relating to Brendan are two Latin documents — *Vita Brendani* (Life of Brendan) and *Navigatio Brendani* (Voyage of Brendan). The *Navigatio* in particular is a work of great literary merit, a tale of the wonders of the sea, rich with the sea-lore of Ireland and western Europe. The *Navigatio Brendani* has been described as the epic of the old Irish Church.

Brendan was born in Kerry in 484 on the Fenit Peninsula, north of the Bay of Tralee. He was a direct descendant of Fergus MacRoy, King of Ireland in the first century. His parents were Christian. Brendan spent his early years in the magnificent Fenit countryside and then, according to the custom of the time, he was sent for fosterage to a famous school for boys which was founded by St Ita. He spent five years at Ita's school, and was so impressed by her teaching that he frequently sought her advice in later life.

After this, Brendan attended the monastic school of Bishop Erc, a forerunner of the great monastic settlements of Clonmacnois and Glendalough. Even at this early date, monastic schools had reached an exceptionally high standard. The activities in the school included weaving, food production and the study of Celtic art for church adornment. There were *scriptoria* in which the sacred books were copied, and these were well equipped with wax tablets, pens, ink horns and leather covers for the precious books.

Here Brendan learned Latin, history, mathematics and astronomy, and it is probable that Gaelic, Greek and Hebrew were also included in the curriculum. His introduction to astronomy and to the construction of boats (which was one of the activities carried out in Bishop Erc's school) must have been of great assistance to him in the later development of his skill as a navigator. In short, this school laid a balanced emphasis on both manual skills and wide scholarship.

Fr John Ryan, in his great work, *Irish Monasticism*, has pointed out that 'Work, whether of agriculture or craftmanship, was the monk's universal law. The cook and the baker, and, no doubt, the carpenter and the smith, were constantly occupied, whilst chariots or boats might require to be got ready for a journey'.

Having completed his studies at Bishop Erc's school, Brendan decided to travel in order to gain new knowledge. At first he spent a period studying scripture, then he wrote his own monastic rule which has long been lost and of which little is now known. He then set out on his first missionary wanderings in Ireland. He made long journeys on foot, and eventually returned to be ordained by Bishop Erc.

Following his ordination, Brendan gathered together a group of followers and they all lived the monastic life according to his rule. Already, Brendan realised that he wanted to sail the seas and he visited the Aran Islands to discuss his project with St Enda. He then returned to his monastery in Tralee and fasted and prayed with his companions for forty days. He built an oratory on the peak of Sliabh Diadche which has since been known as Sides Brendani — the Seat of Brendan. This oratory consisted of a hut of stones with a reed mat for a bed. The lamp which gave him light burned on the oil of basking-sharks. He had a leather satchel for his books.

As soon as Brendan came down from the mountain he began to build a boat in preparation for a voyage. This boat was a great currach — its hull was covered with three layers of oak-tanned hides. Its joints were sealed with holly resin and it was then waterproofed. It was then fitted with a sail made from the hides

The Brendan Voyage

of animals. Brendan put stores of food and other necessities for the voyage on board. The food was packed in earthenware jars and consisted mainly of dried fish, grain and root crops. It is not certain how many monks sailed with Brendan on this voyage, but all of them were experienced sailors.

They set their course to the north-west, and after more than a month at sea they saw land. Their supplies had already been exhausted, but the uninviting land before them was craggy and barren. It was the island of St Kilda, in the farthest Hebrides. Half-mad with thirst, they sailed round the rugged island for three days before finding a safe landing-place. Then they rested and restocked their supplies. Brendan's cell can still be seen on St Kilda and Hebridean fishermen still invoke a form of his name, Branuilt, when they are in danger at sea.

Brendan's next port of call was one of the Faroe Islands. He is said to have landed at a bay in the Island of Storms, and he was remembered here until the Middle Ages. Even as late as 1420 a

17

church called Brendansvik was dedicated to him. A round tower, built as a memorial to the expedition, still survives on one of the Faroe Islands.

After the sailors had left the Faroes they didn't sight anything for several weeks. Then they saw something which loked like a small island, and disembarked to celebrate the Easter feast. They had just lit a great fire, fanned by exposure to strong winds, when suddenly the island lurched as if there had been an earthquake, and began to sink under the water. The terrified monks had barely enough time to get aboard their boat again. They had landed on the back of a sleeping whale!

Brendan and his crew were then blown on an erratic course south-east from the Faroes. They finally sighted menacing cliffs about six hundred feet high towering out of the angry sea. This was the uninhabited island of Noss in the Shetlands, and they rested, replenished their stores and celebrated Pentecost there.

Afterwards, according to O'Hanlon's *Lives of the Saints*, 'they sailed for three months, seeing nothing but sea and sky, only eating once in every two or three days'. At length they saw another craggy island, and having sailed up a narrow fiord, they moored their boat. They were met by a white-bearded monk, Aibiu, who took them to his monastery. When the delighted monks had eaten and exchanged reminiscences, they all went to pray in the oratory. This was a square building, and the altars and sacred vessels were made from crystal. The community to which Aibiu belonged had lived on this remote northern island of the Shetlands for eighty years.

After this the sailors encountered some dreadful weather. There were gales, hail and lightning, and it was probably at this time that one of the monks wrote that 'the sky, it seems, would pour down stinking pitch'. It is said that the sailors landed on a number of other remote islands and celebrated Christmas before eventually reaching Iceland. Here they were greeted by the sight of the volcano Hecla in eruption, and when one of the party went ashore a stream of lava engulfed him. Brendan was horrified, and he instructed his companions to 'shake out more sail, and put your backs into those oars that we may go from this place'.

They visited a number of other northern islands, and when the

St Brendan's boat meets the icebergs and the walruses

Easter celebrations were over, they weighed anchor and set sail for Ireland. It is said that Brendan came ashore at night by the light of a candle kept burning every night by a lay-brother who refused to believe that the sailors were lost. Brendan had been at sea for five years and his friends, with the exception of the lay-brother, had mourned him as if he were dead. Brendan went to visit his foster-mother, Ita. She warned him that he must not put to sea in a haphazard manner any more, but that he must build a wooden boat and navigate with the help of a written sailing guide. After spending some time in Ireland, Brendan began to feel restless again and decided to go on another voyage, this time in a boat that was probably made of oak.

Again, Brendan first went to visit his friend St Enda in Aran, where he remained for one month. It is thought that he left

Ireland with his companions on 22 March 551. They sailed west for forty days into an ocean region of dense fog. The air suddenly became cold, and then the monks saw a large iceberg. They described it as the 'colour of silver, harder than marble, of substance of the clearest crystal'. Brendan and his crew were so fascinated by the sculptured shapes of the great iceberg that they spent three days watching it. They were also fascinated by the sight of unusual sea creatures with 'cat-like heads, eyes of the colour of a bronze cauldron, fuzzy pelts, boars' tusks, and heavy spotted bellies'. These creatures were probably walruses, and the available evidence indicates that at that time Brendan was sailing close to the coast of Newfoundland. However, the sailors, distrustful of the general appearance of the area and somewhat alarmed by the unfamiliar barks of the walruses, decided not to go ashore. They continued their voyage, coasting southwards. One of Brendan's crew, Crosan, the king's jester, fell ill and died, and was buried on the shore of a sheltered bay. He is probably the first Irishman to have been buried in the New World. Soon afterwards, one of the men who had helped to build the boat died, and Brendan decided that his good friend should be buried at sea. This is the first recorded Christian burial at sea in the history of northern Europe.

As the boat sailed on it entered warmer waters where the travellers saw a water-spout sparkling violet, green, yellow and orange in the sunlight. Soon a headland with palm trees growing on its shore appeared. When the voyagers had cast anchor on the coral shore, a group of pygmies whose language they did not understand waved their weapons at the sailors. It is believed that this was one of the Bahama Islands. Despite the threats of the hostile islanders, the ship remained anchored on the beautiful tropical island for seven days. However, Brendan forbade his crew to go ashore for fear they would be forced to fight. When they decided to set sail again, they discovered that the anchor was stuck in a coral reef and they were unable to free it. They left without it and one of the crew later made another one.

A short time later they landed on one of the largest of the Bahama Islands, where, as on the Faroe Islands, they were met by a very old man wearing ragged leather clothes. He told

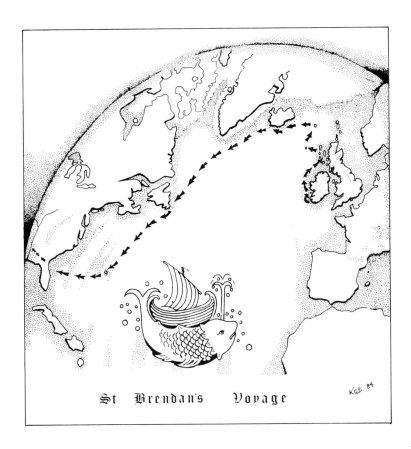

St Brendan's Voyage

Kel. 84

Brendan that he had also come from Ireland and had lived on the island for a very long time. His home was a little stone oratory. There had been twelve men in his community at first, but one by one they had died from old age or illness. He advised Brendan not to stay in the place for too long, and warned him of the danger of sharks in the surrounding waters.

The ship had travelled only a short distance from the shore when it was attacked by a man-eating shark. This was a completely new experience for Brendan's crew who had never encountered a dangerous sea-creature before. However, as the shark circled the boat, it was attacked by another monstrous creature — probably a great ray — and they fought viciously until they killed each other.

The old hermit had watched the great fight from the shore, and when he waved his arms in delight at the escape of Brendan and his crew, they decided to return to him. They soon realised that he was close to death, and Brendan administered the last sacraments to him. When he had died peacefully, the sailors left the island once again.

This time they sailed into a calm blue sea where they were charmed by the sight of many unusual and beautiful sea birds and fishes. When they reached coral sands 'it seemed as if they could touch with their hands its greatest depth, and the fishes were visible in great shoals like flocks of sheep in the pastures'. They spent eight days in this enchanting sea, and eventually they anchored on the white sands of such a beautiful country that they were convinced that they had found the Land of Promise of Saints. From their descriptions of the place, it seems that they had landed near Miami Beach. Here they felt they had reached the end of their journey, and they were overjoyed at the beautiful countryside which surrounded them, 'a land odorous, flower-smooth, blessed. A land many-melodied, musical, shouting for joy, unmournful'. Again, to their amazement, they met a very old Irish monk, Festivas, who told them that he had lived there for thirty years. He told them what he knew about the country in which they had landed, and advised Brendan to explore the land and its people.

Brendan immediately made preparations for a land expedition. He and his companions travelled for forty days, until they came to a wide river. They were unable to cross this river and camped on its bank where they rested and discussed their plans for the future. The river may have been the Mississippi or one of its tributaries. While they were resting, another stranger, who may have been a local Indian, came to visit them and after discussion with him Brendan decided not to explore any further, but to return to his ship. It must be remembered that he understood that the land-mass on which he had landed was another island rather than a continent. They spent some more time with Festivas and his companions and then Brendan

22

decided that he would return to Ireland. It is not clear why he made this decision, having already visited so many places in which he could have set up a missionary settlement.

Around 553 Brendan and his crew said goodbye to Festivas. They renewed their stores with fruit in Florida and brought gold and precious stones with them to adorn the sacred vessels in Ireland. They arrived back in the Aran Islands after an absence of two years, and told the story of their latest expedition to St Enda and his community.

Brendan then sailed southwards to the Shannon Estuary, and he soon began to make missionary journeys in Ireland with as much zeal as he had previously employed in sailing the uncharted waters. He is said to have built churches in Connaught, Munster and Leinster. The fame of his voyages had already spread throughout Ireland, and many churches and shrines were dedicated to him. He founded his chief monastery at Clonfert, west of the Shannon above Lough Derg. He also founded a number of other monasteries on islands on the Shannon and Lough Corrib, and it is believed that he was appointed Bishop and had episcopal authority over Clonfert.

The fame of Brendan's seafaring adventures spread over the centuries until the story of his voyages became a part of European literature. As far as it is known, Brendan himself did not write any account of his voyages — the only surviving work attributed to him is a long litany-like prayer known as the Prayer of St Brendan. However, the influence of his voyages was reflected for centuries by the number of Irishmen who sailed to remote islands and lived there as hermits. Traces of Celtic civilisation which have been found throughout northern Europe and America have been attributed by scholars to the influence of these Irishmen whose names have never been recorded. Perhaps others, such as Columbanus, who led a more active missionary life were also stimulated by the story of Brendan's great search for the Land of Promise.

It is said that Brendan's last voyage was a journey of penance, during the course of which he visited a number of Scottish islands, including Iona. Several churches in Scotland bear his name as patron and it is therefore likely that he preached

23

Christianity there twenty years before the arrival of Colmcille. Brendan spent three years in Scotland and revisited it when he was eighty, accompanied by three other great Irish teachers — Comgall of Bangor, Canice of Kilkenny and Cormac of Durrow. They visited Colmcille on the Island of Hinba, close to Iona. Adamnan, Colmcille's biographer, declared that 'Brendan was the greatest founder of monasteries of them all'. Colmcille referred to his meeting with Brendan in one of his songs: 'and Brendan, the truthful, is there in the west...'.

Brendan left Scotland and went to Wales where he met Gildas the Wise, a great scholar who had been educated in Armagh. He stayed with Gildas for some time, and then went to study with another Welsh scholar and scribe, Cadoc of Llancarvan. He lived with Cadoc for a period of retreat, then built a cell on the banks of the Severn, near the present city of Bristol.

Brendan then visited Brittany where his former chief officer, Machutus (after whom the town of St Malo is named), had built a monastery at Alyth, a great headland near the mouth of the Rance River. This area of Brittany is renowned for the rugged splendour of its coastline. Brendan built his oratory on the great crag of Cezembre. Today, there is a stone chapel nearby which has inscriptions honouring him over the altar: 'Merci à St Brendan' and 'Hommage à St Brendan'. A heart and an anchor are carved over these inscriptions. According to the ninth century historian, Bili, Clerk of Alet, Gildas of Wales and King Arthur of Cornwall joined Machutus and Brendan to help spread Christianity in the area.

Brendan's last voyages, which he made as a pilgrim missionary rather than a great navigator, are perhaps the most astounding of all. He is said to have visited the Canary Islands, and to have planted a laurel bush there which was venerated in his memory for many years. A shrine in his honour was erected in Tenerife. His next journey took him to Egypt, from where he went on to Greece and sailed through the islands of the Aegean.

When Brendan was over ninety years of age he returned to his monastic foundation at Clonfert, which had become one of the great seats of learning in Ireland. He went to visit his sister Bríd in her convent in Annaghduin and died there on 16 May 577. He was buried in his own monastic foundation of Clonfert.

The story of St Brendan and his voyages still fascinates people today. It captured the imagination of the explorer Tim Severin to such an extent that he decided to undertake a voyage in a primitive craft following as far as possible Brendan's route as described in the *Navigatio*. Using only the materials that were available in Brendan's day, Severin and his companions made a boat with a wooden frame tied together with leather thongs. It had a skin of oak bark leather stitched together with flax and protected with wool grease. A crew of five sailed it across the Atlantic via the Hebrides, the Faroes, Iceland and along the coast of Greenland until they reached Newfoundland, thus proving that much of the legend of St Brendan might be true, and Severin himself believes that St Brendan was just one of a number of Irish monks who travelled far into the Atlantic and brought back news of the countries they had visited. It is therefore probable that St Brendan and his seafaring companions reached America hundreds of years before the Vikings, and nearly a thousand years before Columbus. Tim Severin named his boat 'Brendan', and the story of his epic adventure is called *The Brendan Voyage*.

25

3

ST COLMCILLE

'That man is little to be envied whose patriotism would not gain force upon the plain of Marathon, or whose piety would not grow warmer among the ruins of Iona'. This was the comment of Dr Samuel Johnson when he had explored the ruins of St Colmcille's church on the rugged, windswept island of Iona.

St Colmcille was a man of many parts. He was scribe and scholar, poet and prophet, as well as being a great missionary. There is more authentic information available about the life of Colmcille than about any of the other early Irish saints. Records of his work and personality were written by three eminent churchmen who lived in the century following his death. Two of these lives were written by Abbots of Iona, one by Ailbe, Abbot from 657-669, and the other by Adamnan, Abbot from 679-704. Adamnan's life has been described as 'perhaps the most valuable document of the Irish Church which has escaped the ravages of time' (Reeves). It was written at the request of the community in Iona and its style and literary finish are an indication of the scholarship that existed in Colmcille's monastery. The third life of Colmcille is by the Venerable Bede, author of *The Ecclesiastical History of the English Nation,* a very valuable sourcebook of the history of England. Bede's scientific approach to the writing of history and biography, making full use of existing records and the testimony of eye-witnesses, was far superior to the general methods of his day. He had considerable contact with the Irish missionaries, and his life of Colmcille is thus of great importance in analysing the contribution of Irish monks to the spread of Christianity and scholarship in Scotland and Northern England.

Columba, or Colmcille, as he is more widely known, was born at Gartan in Donegal in 563. He was a prince of the royal Uí

Néill family, and had he not chosen to be a monk, it is possible that he would have become High King of Ireland. When he was old enough to leave his foster-father, Cruithnechan, he decided to study under the greatest scholars in Ireland. First he went to Moville in the north of the Inishowen peninsula to study scripture under the founder, St Finian, and he later learned the art of poetry from a bard known as Master Gemman. Colmcille himself wrote a considerable amount of verse and was regarded as the saint of the *fili* (bards).

When he had finished his training as a bard, Colmcille went to Clonard in County Meath where another St Finian was Abbot. Because of his broad knowledge of the scriptures which he had gained in Ireland and Wales, this Finian was known as 'Teacher of the saints of Eire'. It is said that about three thousand monks lived in Clonard at the height of its fame, and many distinguished founders of Celtic and Continental churches were

St Columbcille's, Churchtown, Co. Donegal, near the Saint's birthplace at Gartan. Traditionally emigrants paid a visit to this site on the evening before leaving Ireland as they believed it would prevent loneliness

educated there. According to the *Martyrology of Donegal,* it was from among these monks that the twelve apostles of Ireland were chosen. Colmcille built his hut near the church, and helped his fellow students to grind corn at a quern.

Having completed his studies at Clonard, Colmcille went to the school of St Mobhi at Glasnevin, where he was ordained a priest. The community broke up during a plague in Glasnevin around 544, and Colmcille returned to his homeland in Donegal. Soon afterwards his cousin, Aodh Mac Ainmireach, High King of Ireland, invited him to his fortress at Aileach. The learned men of the north and the best poets, musicians and entertainers gathered to greet him. Aodh drove him in his chariot to an island on the Foyle on which splendid oak trees grew. 'This island is yours', said Aodh, 'I wish you to found your monastery here'.

So Colmcille founded his famous monastery of Derry, and formed his first community. Derry, from the Irish *doire,* means a 'place of oaks', and Colmcille built his church on the high hill among the oak trees. Later, Colmcille wrote a poem in praise of Derry:

> Dearly I love Derry for
> Its gentle fields and brightness,
> And the fair angelic host
> Filling it with lightness.

The work of the monks was domestic, agricultural and cultural. The monastery had a guest house for pilgrims and travellers. Colmcille's monastery in Derry survived for many centuries after his death. It was destroyed several times by the Danes, but was restored on each occasion.

According to some authorities, Colmcille founded three hundred monasteries in Ireland. This seems improbable, and there are no records to substantiate this. However, he did found two monasteries in his native province, one at Raphoe, and one on windswept Tory Island. The remains of a round tower attached to this monastery still stand on the island. There was also a famous round tower at Swords. In Colmcille's foundations at Kells and Durrow the scribes perfected the art of illumination and the two greatest examples of the art, the Books of Kells and

Durrow, were produced at these great monasteries. Happily, both codices have survived and are now housed in Trinity College, Dublin. The monastery at Kells served as a refuge for the monks of Iona when they were driven out during the Norse persecutions. Colmcille sang the praises of his foundations:

> Beloved are Durrow and Derry,
> Beloved is Raphoe the pure,
> Beloved are Swords and Kells,
> But sweeter and fairer to me
> The salt sea, where the sea gulls cry —
> When I come to Derry from far,
> It is sweeter and dearer to me.

Colmcille was patron and protector of the bards in Ireland, and they were always welcome at his monasteries. He himself wrote in Latin and Irish, and collections of poems attributed to him or relating to him are still preserved in the Bodleian Library at Brussels. Some of these poems are of considerable literary merit, and are noteworthy for depicting the Irish characteristic of appreciation and observation of nature. Many of his poems written in exile in Iona praised the charms of Ireland.

There is a certain amount of confusion surrounding the reason for Colmcille's departure from Ireland. Some scholars say that his decision to leave was purely his own, while others say that he was forced to do so because he was held in some way responsible for the batttle of Cuil Dreimhne near Sligo in 561. This battle appears to have been the result of the stubbornness and pride of two of Ireland's greatest men of learning, Colmcille himself, and his former teacher, Finian of Moville. Finian had gone on a pilgrimage to Rome and brought back a copy of the Gospels written by St Jerome. When Colmcille heard about it he asked Finian's permission to copy this excellent version of the scriptures. Finian refused as he wished to be the sole possessor of such a rare and precious work. Colmcille remained at Finian's monastery for some time and secretly made a complete copy of the book. When Finian found out what Colmcille had done, he demanded the copy of the book, insisting that as the original was his, so also was the copy. Colmcille refused to part with his copy, and the dispute was referred to Diarmuid, the High King of Ireland, who was bound by oath to make a just decision on all disputes that were brought before him.

Colmcille argued that the mere fact of his having copied the book did not cause any loss to Finian. On the contrary, it would help spread knowledge among the people. Diarmuid's famous verdict on the case is well-known: 'To every book belongs its son-book, as to every cow belongs her calf'. Colmcille decided to avenge this judgment, and the dispute was further aggravated when the King of Connacht's son was killed by the High King's soldiers after he had taken refuge in Colmcille's church.

Colmcille returned to his native Donegal in a rage. The Uí Néill armies came to his assistance and defeated the High King's army at Cuil Dreimhne, near Sligo town. As in all battles, there was no real victor. Because of the bloodshed, Colmcille was disgraced, and was censured by both the civil and eccleciastical authorities. The book at the centre of the dispute was afterwards known as the *Catach,* or book of battle. Encased in silver, it was held by the O'Donnell clan for many years. In 1497 it was seized by the MacDermotts, and it is now in the museum of the Royal Irish Academy in Dublin.

Following the defeat of the High King a synod was convened at Telltown in County Meath at which Molaise of Devenish presided. It is said that Molaise imposed a sentence of perpetual exile on Colmcille for his misdeed.

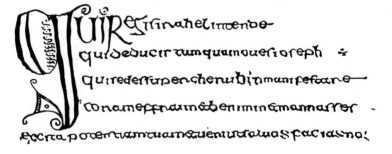

Cathac Colmcille – The Battle Book of St Colmcille (sample of script)

Reconstruction of Monastery of Iona as it may have been about the time of St Colmcille

Colmcille decided to go to Scotland. He seems to have had two motives for his choice: firstly, he wanted to spread Christianity; and secondly, he wished to bring about peaceful relations between the Irish colony of Dal Riada and their more powerful overlords, the Picts. At this time, the Picts ruled the greater part of Scotland and northern England. About sixty years previously, the Irish kings of the Dal Riada line (who were related to Colmcille) had colonised a portion of the west of Scotland. However, they had recently been defeated by the Picts, and their Scottish possessions were in danger.

Colmcille left Ireland in 563 when he was forty-two years old. He sailed towards Scotland, or Alba, as it was then known, accompanied by twelve companions. They sailed from Lough Foyle in a currach and landed on Iona, about twelve miles from the Scottish mainland. Iona is separated from the mainland by a mile-wide channel. Its shores are bleak and covered in sand, and

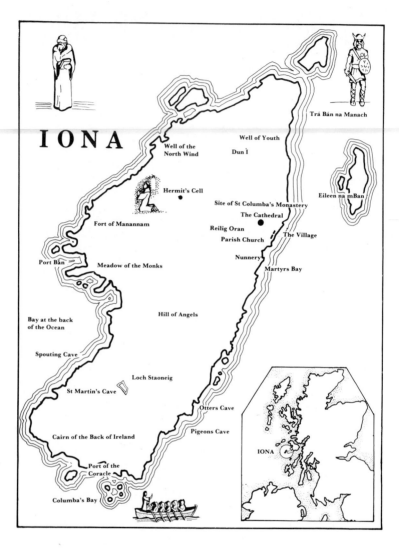

IONA

Trá Bán na Manach

Well of the North Wind

Well of Youth

Dun Ì

Hermit's Cell

Eileen na mBan

Site of St Columba's Monastery

The Cathedral

Fort of Manannam

Reilig Oran

Parish Church

The Village

Port Bán

Meadow of the Monks

Nunnery

Martyrs Bay

Hill of Angels

Bay at the back of the Ocean

Spouting Cave

Loch Staoneig

St Martin's Cave

Otters Cave

Cairn of the Back of Ireland

Pigeons Cave

IONA

Port of the Coracle

Columba's Bay

some are broken into great cliffs. The bay where Colmcille cast anchor has been known as 'Port na Churaich' since then. According to the Annals of Tighearnach, the island was donated to Colmcille by his relative, Conall, King of the Irish Scots of

32

northern Britain. Immediately after landing, Colmcille set about building a number of huts in wattle and wood. He later built a more permanent monastery, which was for many years the chief seminary of Great Britain and the burial place of the kings of Scotland and of many monks and scholars. When Dr Johnson visited Iona, he said that 'we are now treading that illustrious island which was once the luminary of the Caledonian regions, whence savage clans and roving barbarians derived the benefits of knowledge and the blessing of religion'.

Colmcille's poetry at this time emphasised his deep regret at leaving Ireland:

> Ah, how my boat would fly if its prow were turned to my Irish oak-grove. But the noble sea now carries me to Albyn, the land of ravens. My foot is in my little boat, but my sad heart ever bleeds. There is a grey eye which ever turns to Erin.

In the meantime, the number of Colmcille's followers in Iona began to increase. The life and discipline of the monastic system closely resembled that of the schools of Finian of Clonard and Comhgall of Bangor.

The monastery comprised a chapel, a dormitory, a kitchen, a hospital and an area for the preservation of both spiritual and general books. Outside there was a cow byre, a barn and a grain storehouse. Strong monks were responsible for agricultural work, while elderly monks transcribed the scriptures and accompanied Colmcille on his walks. Colmcille's own hut had been built with planks on an elevated area. When he had established himself on the island, he prepared his rule, which has been translated by the great Irish scholar Eugene O'Curry from the manuscript in the Burgundian Library in Brussels. 'Three labours in the day', declared Colmcille, 'prayers, work and reading'. Baoithin was Colmcille's chief scribe, and he excelled at the ornamentation of manuscripts, especially the sacred writings. The name Baoithin is immortalised in a beautiful Gaelic script devised by the Irish typefounder and publisher Colm Ó Lochlainn and used in many excellent examples of fine printing in Gaelic.

When he had organised the monastery on Iona, Colmcille

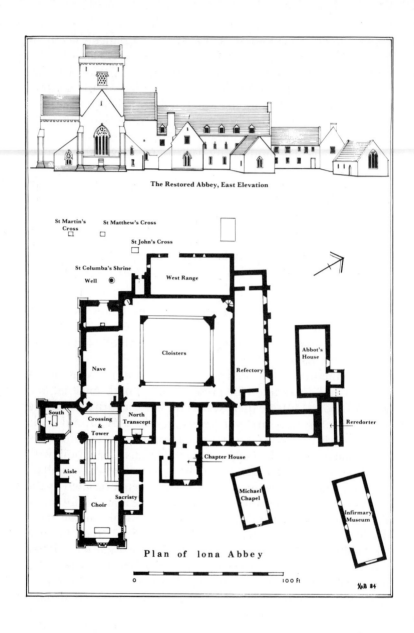

The Restored Abbey, East Elevation

St Martin's Cross

St Matthew's Cross

St John's Cross

St Columba's Shrine

Well

West Range

Cloisters

Nave

Refectory

Abbot's House

South

Crossing & Tower

North Transcept

Reredorter

Aisle

Chapter House

Michael Chapel

Infirmary Museum

Choir

Sacristy

Plan of Iona Abbey

0   100 ft

KoB 84

decided to expand into the mountainous lands of the Picts. At that time the Picts were ruled by King Brude from his capital near Inverness. Although the monks had spent some time studying the language, they still needed two Picts to travel with them as interpreters. After some opposition Colmcille managed to gain admission to Brude's fortress. It is not known when Brude became a Christian. His foster-father, Broichan, was a magician who used his magical powers to disrupt the work of the monks. Records of Colmcille's work among the Picts are scarce, but we know that the Irish monks had considerable influence in the Pictish kingdom.

When Colmcille returned to Iona he found that his community had grown. He therefore set about organising a system of communication between the principal monastery in Iona and the various foundations on the islands and in Scotland. Iona retained authority over all the new foundations, and for many centuries its Abbot held the power of a primate over the Scottish hierarchy.

Despite the apparent disgrace in which Colmcille left Ireland, he was still remembered there for his ability and diplomacy, and when his cousin, Conall, King of Dal Riada died, he was asked to crown the new king.

In 575 he returned to Ireland for an occasion of special importance — the Convention of Drumceat. Meetings such as this were called every few years by the High King to discuss matters of national importance. According to the ancient tract *Amra Colmcille*, there were three reasons for his visit to Ireland. In the first instance, Colmcille was now regarded as a suitable mediator between the Scots and the Irish in their dispute over the Kingdom of Dal Riada; the second issue concerned the excessive demands of the bards, some of whom were in danger of being banished from Ireland at the time; the third issue concerned the release of a hostage being held by the High King.

The dispute concerning the bards was of particular interest to Colmcille since he himself was a *file* or bard. This dispute was so serious that the High King was considering expelling the bards from his kingdom. The bards had always been an influential class in ancient Ireland and were accustomed to having many

St Martin's Cross 10th Century   **IONA**

36

privileges. Together with the princes and the druids, they took part in the great national assemblies. They ranked next to the monarch himself, and had a fixed title to the chieftains' territory.

However, as the bards grew in number, they became very powerful, and as time went on they began to abuse their power. When the kings and chiefs did not give in to their demands, the bards mocked them with bitter satirical verse.

During the course of the meeting at which their fate was considered, Colmcille took part in a lengthy debate, acting as mediator between the bards and the King. He said that they should be retained, for 'the praises they will sing for you will be enduring as the praises sung for Cormac were'. It was finally decided to reduce the number of bards and to limit their demands. Thereafter, the bards flourished at the courts of kings, and were shown hospitality by the chieftains for many centuries.

This was one of Colmcille's last visits to Ireland. Many people wanted to meet him again, and as he and his friends returned from the Convention great crowds of people carrying gifts turned out to greet them along the way.

After this, with the exception of a few short visits to Ireland, Colmcille spent the rest of his missionary life founding monasteries among the islands surrounding Iona. His biographer, Adamnan, gives us little information regarding dates and places, referring to Colmcille simply as 'the father and founder of monasteries, that within the territories of the Picts and the Scots'.

In 584 Colmcille's work expanded to a new area in the territory of the southern Picts. Christianity had been practised here previously, but the people had gradually fallen away from it. King Brude's successor, Gertnaidh, founded a new monastic church which became the headquarters of Colmcille's monks. In this mission Colmcille was assisted by Cainneach, a monk of Pictish descent, who appears to have been the founder of a monastery in east Fife on the same site on which the Church of St Andrew was later founded.

Colmcille returned to Ireland for a short time in 585. He visited his monastery in Durrow, and then went to the great monastic school of Clonmacnois. The Abbot, monks and students gave him an enthusiastic welcome, and he must certainly have been delighted by the atmosphere surrounding Iona.

Colmcille spent a total of thirty-four years in northern Britain. During that time he founded Iona, which was to be the most important monastery in Britain for centuries. The monks of Iona were renowned navigators, and explored the bays, gulfs and caverns around the rugged coast of Scotland. They were skilled fishermen, and provided food from the seas for the poor people they met on their travels. An old Irish poem pays tribute to the seafaring missionaries:

> Honour to the soldiers who live in Iona
> There are three times fifty under the monastic rule
> Seventy of whom are appointed to row
> And cross the sea in their leathern barks.

When the Norwegians began their voyages to the coast of Scotland in search of plunder, they found Celtic books, crosses and bells which were probably the work of the Iona monks.

Colmcille was also succesful on the political front, setting up the dynasty that ruled Dal Riada and Scotland for the next five hundred years. The last years of his life were spent mainly in prayer or in visiting his monks. He was so worn out with age that he sometimes had to be carried in a cart. Many stories of his affection for animals date from this period of his life. Considering the period in which he lived and the important part often played by animals and birds in the lives of the Irish saints, the young Colmcille did not often show great tenderness towards them. However, two stories of his affection for animals are among the best-loved in Irish literature. The first concerns a crane which Colmcille predicted would arrive weary and wind-tossed from Ireland. He told one of his monks to watch out for the bird when it fell upon the shore. 'You will take heed to lift it tenderly and carry it to the house nearby, and having taken it in as a guest there you will wait upon it for three days and nights, and feed it with anxious care'. The brother did as he was told and after three days the bird winged its way back to Ireland.

One day, as Colmcille was going from the monastery to the barn, he sat down to rest. Adamnan tells us that 'a white horse came to him, the obedient servant acccustomed to carry the milk vessels between the pasture and the monastery. Knowing that its master would eventualy depart from it, and that it would see him no more, it began to mourn, and like a human being to let tears fall freely on the lap of the saint, and foaming much, to weep aloud'. One of the monks tried to drive the horse away, but Colmcille forbade him. 'Let it alone as it is so fond of me', he said. Then Colmcille blessed the old work-horse, and turned away from him sadly.

He prophesied about his monastery as follows: 'Small and mean as this place is, yet it shall be held in great and unusual honour, not only by Scotic kings and people, but also by rulers of foreign and barbarous nations and their subjects'. Then he spent some time at work at which he excelled — transcribing the scriptures. When he came to Psalm 34 he wrote: 'here at this page I must stop, and what follows let Baoithin write'. When the bell rang for Matins the following morning Colmcille went to the church, and moments later he was found lying in front of the altar where he died. Many years later, when the Danes plundered Alba, the monks brought Colmcille's body back to Ireland and had it buried in Downpatrick beside St Patrick and St Brigid.

St Columcille, St Columbanus and St Brendan crossed oceans and made long, dangerous journeys. Historians have accepted that the Irish had an instinct for the dramatic and often the extreme in spreading Christianity. They risked their lives, they fasted and they made tremendous demands on their companions and fellow missionaries, but it can be said that the Irish revived the spirit of the early Church. When these early Irish missionaries had come and gone, the Benedictine Order founded by St Benedict of Nursia with its emphasis on 'daily prayer, daily bread and daily work' (Cardinal Newman) spread throughout Europe. This monastic movement was followed some centuries later by the rise of the great contemplative orders — the Cistercians and the Carthusians.

4

ST MALACHY Ó MORGAIR

St Malachy is perhaps best known as the patron saint of the diocese of Down and Connor. This famous bishop had the great advantage of having his biography written by one of the greatest fathers of the western Church, St Bernard, Abbot of the Cistercian monastery of Clairvaux in France. Bernard and Malachy were close friends, and Bernard wrote the biography at the request of the Abbot Congan, who had charge of one of the Cistercian communities sent over to Ireland by Bernard. St Malachy was not a missionary in the strictest sense of the word, rather an eminent churchman and reformer who was successful in introducing the Cistercians and their contemplative way of life to the Irish Church.

Malachy O Morgair was born in 1094, probably in the city of Armagh. St Bernard tells us that his parents 'were by birth and power great, such as the world calls great'. According to the *Annals of Inisfallen,* Malachy's father was Mughron Ó Morgair, 'chief lector of Armagh and of all the west of Europe'. His mother's family owned the lands of the great monastic school at Bangor. It is thought that there were at least three children, two sons and a daughter, in the family. The eldest boy, Giolla-Chriost, became Bishop of Clogher. The *Annals of the Four Masters* describe Malachy as a 'paragon of wisdom and piety, a brilliant lamp that enlightened the laity and clergy by preaching and good deeds'.

When Malachy was about eight years old, his father died, and his mother made every effort to obtain the best teachers for the boy. While he was still a young man Malachy placed himself under the protection of Ivor O' Hagan, a hermit renowned for his piety.

After some years, Celsus, Archbishop of Armagh, conferred the order of deacon on Malachy, even though he had not yet reached the canonical age of twenty-five years. It is believed that he was ordained around 1119. Celsus appointed him his vicar and put him in charge of correcting the many abuses that had taken root in the diocese. It seems strange that these abuses should have developed in the wake of the Golden Age of Christianity in Ireland and after early Irish monks had played such a prominent role in spreading Christianity throughout western Europe.

Various reasons have been put forward for this lack of discipline in the medieval Irish Church. The most important single factor was undoubtedly the Viking invasions during which the great monastic schools were attacked and burned, the monks put to death, sacred vessels carried away, and the famous illuminated books in which the gospels were recorded ripped from their protective caskets and destroyed. These invasions continued for several centuries until the Danes were finally defeated and their power in Ireland brought to an end by King Brian Boru at the great Battle of Clontarf in 1014. There were other reasons for the laxity in the Irish Church, among them feuds between rival kings and princes, the complicated system of lay ownership of monastic lands, and lay control over the appointment of abbots.

St Bernard reminds us of the many abuses which Malachy set about reforming while he was vicar of Armagh. Among his reforms were the revival of frequent confession and the regular administering of confirmation. He was also instrumental in restoring the sacred chant and in regularising certain practices relating to the sacrament of marriage. In order to ensure that his reforms were within the laws of the universal Church, Malachy placed himself under the instruction of Malchus, the learned Bishop of Lismore.

On his return from Lismore, Malachy established a monastic community in Bangor over which he was appointed Abbot. At that time the celebrated monastery was in the ruins to which it had been reduced by the Danes, but its extensive possessions were still held by the *Coarbs,* the successors of St Comhgall.

Malachy brought ten companions with him and had soon built a fine wooden oratory at Bangor.

In 1124 Malachy was appointed Bishop of Connor although he was only thirty years old. Connor was in need of many reforms after the devastation of the area surrounding Carlingford Lough by the Viking invaders. Its schools and monasteries had been burned down, its clergy massacred and its monastic libraries burned. This long struggle with the Vikings had also resulted in laxity in the practice of the Christian faith.

St Bernard provides us with a detailed discussion of these abuses and of the many measures taken by Malachy to correct them. He also describes many of the miracles which were attributed to Malachy from this period until the end of his life. Malachy visited the most remote villages and rural areas in his new diocese, always travelling by foot. He was usually accompanied on these journeys by a group of Bangor monks — his main residence at this time was Bangor. In or around 1129 the city of Connor was destroyed by an Irish king and Malachy was forced to flee from his diocese and go to Munster with 120 monks. They took refuge with King Cormac of Desmond who gave them a site for a monastery in his kingdom. He also helped them to build and furnish the monastery, and appointed Malachy his spiritual adviser. Although he was a bishop, Malachy assisted the monks in their various duties in the monastery, such as serving at table or reading and chanting in church. It is not certain where this monastery was situated, but it is believed to have been at Iveragh in County Kerry. As soon as it was safe to do so, Malachy returned to his northern monastery of Bangor. It is thought that his companion monks went with him and the monastery of Iveragh ceased to function.

At about this time Celsus, Archbishop of Armagh, was taken ill and made a will indicating that Malachy was to succeed him in the See of Armagh. However, after Celsus' death the archdiocese was taken over by an interloper, Maurice, and for five years Malachy was forced to live outside Armagh, carrying on his pastoral and reforming work from there.

The *Annals of the Four Masters* record that in 1132 'Mael-maedhog Ua Morgair sat in the successorship of St Patrick at the request of the clergy of Ireland'. However, it was 1134 before Malachy entered Armagh as its Archbishop and Primate of all Ireland.

In 1136 he resigned his position and returned to his former diocese of Down. He founded a monastery at Downpatrick and again set about reorganising certain aspects of the Irish Church. He felt that the palium should be obtained for the Archbishops of Armagh and Cashel, and decided to go to Rome to place his request before the Pope. He travelled to Scotland, then to York, where a pious nobleman gave him his own horse for the journey. He then went to France where he stopped at Clairvaux and met St Bernard, who was so impressed by his character and work that he decided to write Malachy's biography. 'To me also in this life', he wrote, 'it was given to me to see this man, in his look and word I was refreshed, and I rejoiced as in all manner of riches'.

Bernard was a Burgundian nobleman who had renounced his inheritance and entered the monastery of Citeaux with thirty companions in 1112. A few years later he was sent by his abbot to start a monastery in a sunny valley in the Langres plateau. The site of this monastery was Clairvaux, the Valley of Light, and it was later to become famous because of Abbot Bernard, because of the saints who were members of the monastic community and because of the great twelfth-century revival of mysticism which took place there. This spiritual renaissance had widespread effects due to Bernard's great influence in the Europe of his day. He left his mark on Gregorian chant, on clerical life and on the whole development of Gothic architecture and art. He too was a reformer of abbeys and a peacemaker, as well as being the preacher of the Second Crusade. His influence led Malachy to bring the Cistercian Order to Ireland. Despite almost continual ill-health and his responsibilities as founder of many monasteries, Bernard was also a great spiritual writer known as 'Doctor Mellifluus', literally, 'the doctor flowing with honey'. Among his most charming and readable works is his biography of St Malachy, whom he held in such high esteem.

When Malachy left Clairvaux he travelled to Rome and was received by Pope Innocent II. His first petition to the Pope was that he be allowed to resign from the See of Armagh and retire to

43

Clairvaux, but this request was not granted. He stayed in Rome for a month visiting the shrines and holy places and he reported to the Pope on his work for the reformation of the Irish Church. Innocent was pleased with the work Malachy had done in his native country, and appointed him Apostolic Delegate in Ireland. However, when he applied for the palium for the dioceses of Armagh and Cashel, the Pope explained to him that he must go about this application in a different way. 'Summon the bishops and clergy and chiefs of the country', the Pope advised, 'hold a general council, and by a vote of the assembly apply for the palium, and it will be granted to you'. The Pope then gave him gifts of sacred vestments and he set out on his return journey to Ireland.

Malachy again travelled by Clairvaux where he explained to Bernard that he had not been given permission to join the Cistercian Order. However, he left five of his companions behind to be trained by Bernard, so that they could form the nucleus of a Cistercian monastery in Ireland. After his return to Ireland he sent others to become monks at Clairvaux.

According to the *Annals of Inisfallen* Malachy returned to his monastery at Bangor in 1140 and immediately took up his duties as Apostolic Delegate. He arranged synods in various parts of the country to reform and regulate the Church in Ireland and he travelled widely throughout the country. Meanwhile, he kept up his contact with Bernard, who dispatched a number of Irish and French Cistercian monks to Ireland in 1142 under the guidance of Abbot Christian, whom he commended as being well versed in the rules of the Order. Malachy had already obtained a suitable site for the new foundation in a pleasant valley in County Louth. Thus was founded the great Abbey of Mellifont which was afterwards renowned for the magnificence of its buildings and for the sanctity and learning of its monks. The progress of the new community was so rapid that in the short space of four years it was able to send its first offshoot to Newry, another a year later to Bective and a third to Boyle in 1148. Cistercian monasteries continued to be founded in Ireland long after Malachy's death.

Mellifont, which took fifteen years to build, was modelled on the mother church at Clairvaux and the new Abbey was the

The Cistercian Abbey of Mellifont, Co. Louth, as it may have appeared about 1225 A.D.

largest in Ireland at the time. All Cistercian monasteries embodied the same general principles of architecture, with the entire monastery arranged in a square surrounding an open green. The consecration ceremony of Mellifont was attended by many kings and nobles, including the High King of Ireland, Muircheartach Ua Lochlainn.

In 1148 Malachy convened a Synod at Skerries in County Dublin. As the paliums had not yet arrived from Rome, and as it was known that Pope Eugene III would shortly be visiting France, it was decided that Malachy should go to meet him there. After the Synod he set out, accompanied as usual by a group of companions. He travelled through Scotland where he founded a Cistercian monastery and was met by King David, the country's ruler. However, due to unforeseen delays on the journey, Malachy was not in time to meet the Pope in France, and decided to continue to Rome to meet him. He rested at Clairvaux, where Bernard was again delighted to meet him. 'On his arrival what a joyous festive day shone on us', Bernard wrote afterwards. Malachy spent four or five very happy days at Clairvaux, but on 18 October he caught a fever and had to take to his bed. At first he was not thought to be seriously ill, but on 2 November he died in the company of St Bernard and his monks. It is believed that Malachy had received the Cistercian habit from Bernard and, in keeping with the monastic custom, he was buried in it in the monastery of Clairvaux. Bernard delivered two funeral orations in honour of his friend.

When Bernard died five years later, his remains were laid beside Malachy's. Their heads are still preserved in the high altar of the Cathedral of Troyes. The Order possesses only small portions of their relics as their shrines were desecrated during the French Revolution. Malachy was canonised in 1190 by Pope Clement III.

The good seed sown at Mellifont took root, and by 1200 there were twenty-six Cistercian abbeys in Ireland, the largest of which was Jerpoint in Kilkenny with 1,300 monks. The Cistercians introduced an advanced system of agriculture and various associated industries to Ireland. The ruins of their many abbeys throughout the country are monuments to the genius of Cistercian architects and builders. At the date of the General Suppression of the Monasteries during the reigns of Henry VIII and Elizabeth I the Order in Ireland consisted of forty-two communities of monks and two of nuns. Its lands, possessions and sacred treasures were confiscated by the Crown, and its priceless libraries were destroyed. Annals and manuscripts which had taken years to compile were torn and burned. The Four Masters lamented that 'from Arran of the Saints to the Iceian sea, there was not one monastery that was not broken or shattered, except a few in Ireland that were not noticed or heeded'. Some of the monks escaped and fled to the Continent, but many others were massacred in their monasteries.

Three centuries later, fleeing from persecutions on the Continent, a group of sixty-four Cistercians landed in Ireland and founded a monastery at Mount Melleray, near Cappoquin in County Waterford. Other foundations included Mount St Joseph's, Roscrea and the new Mellifont, near the site of the original monastery founded by St Malachy. Through these monasteries the influence of Malachy Ó Morgair has come down to us through the ages.

47

5

ST OLIVER PLUNKETT

Sunday, 12 October 1975 was a particularly happy day for the Irish pilgrims who gathered in St Peter's Square in Rome, for on that day a wish of several hundred years was fulfilled when Pope Paul VI solemnly canonised the successor of St Patrick, St Oliver Plunkett. After giving a special welcome to the Irish, the family of St Patrick, the Pope declared that a new saint had been added to the calendar of saints of the Church, 'and this new saint is Oliver Plunkett, bishop and martyr. Oliver Plunkett, successor of St Patrick in the See of Armagh. Oliver Plunkett, glory of Ireland and saint today and forever of the Church of God. Oliver Plunkett for all — for the entire world — an authentic and outstanding example of the love of Christ'.

The Pope went on to outline the suffering experienced by Oliver Plunkett during his life, and to discuss his pastoral activities. He said that he was the advocate of justice and friend of the oppressed but would not compromise truth or condone violence. He referred to the twenty-two years spent by Oliver Plunkett in Rome before he returned to Ireland and to the fact that he had served as chaplain to the Oratorians and had visited the sick in the Hospital of the Holy Spirit, Rome.

The canonisation Mass was celebrated with the Pope by Cardinal Conway, then Archbishop of Armagh, the Archbishops of Dublin, Cashel and Tuam, the Bishop of Meath, of whose diocese Oliver was a native, and the Bishop of Ferns. Many of Oliver's relatives also attended the ceremony. Members of the Plunkett family and of the great Anglo-Irish families, proud of the occasion and of the tradition which linked them to the martyr, had assembled from several countries.

Beautiful canonisation gifts from Ireland were offered during the Mass. A special Mass of St Oliver was prepared and was offered in every parish church in Ireland on the afternoon of the day after the canonisation. In a special ceremony on 1 November a major relic of St Oliver was transferred from Drogheda to his birthplace at Oldcastle, County Meath. Monsignor John Hanley, also a native of Oldcastle, had been Postulator or Promoter of Blessed Oliver's cause and he played an important part in the canonisation ceremonies. He had previously made a detailed study of the life and miracles of the Saint and had edited *The Letters of St Oliver Plunkett 1625-81, Archbishop of Armagh and Primate of all Ireland.* These letters give many interesting insights to the various events and personalities of Oliver's time. He wrote in English, Italian and Latin and gave a clear picture of all matters relating to the Church in Ireland.

Oliver Plunkett was born at Loughcrew near Oldcastle on 1 November 1625. His father was of a well-known Anglo-Irish family and owned a small estate of about 300 acres there and a further 360 acres in neighbouring parishes until the Cromwellian confiscations dispossessed him of most of his lands. He was related to Lords Fingall, Dunsany and Louth. Oliver had one brother, Edward and three sisters, Catherine, Anne and Mary. His cousin, Dr Patrick Plunkett, was Abbot of St Mary's Abbey in Dublin and later Bishop of Ardagh and Meath. He interested himself in Oliver's education and acted as his tutor until the boy was sixteen. It seems likely that Oliver spent part of his childhood in Killeen, the residence of Lord Fingall, and part of it in Dublin in the house of Sir Nicholas Plunkett, Patrick's brother. He was given an excellent grounding in the classics and in the Irish language which he could still speak after living in Rome for almost twenty-five years.

In 1641 there were several uprisings throughout Ulster which spread to many parts of Ireland. These events disrupted Oliver's studies, but Fr Peter Francis Scarampi, Papal Envoy to the Confederation of Kilkenny, took an interest in the boy's welfare, and when Oliver decided to study for the priesthood, Fr Scarampi chose Rome as the ideal place for the further training of his talented pupil. It was therefore decided that Oliver should travel with Fr Scarampi when he returned to Rome in 1647.

49

They sailed from Waterford to Flanders and then set off on a hazardous and wearying journey across Europe. A large part of Flanders and the German states had been devastated by the Thirty Years War, and bands of brigands roamed the countryside. However, the two travellers arrived safely in Paris in late March 1647, and finally reached Rome in May.

It had already been decided that Oliver should study at the famous Irish College founded by Fr Luke Wadding in 1628 for the training of Irish priests. Like all new students at the College, Oliver began his course with an eight-day reatreat, after which he was given his uniform. His own clothes were then sold and the proceeds put into the College funds. He was now an official member of the College community, sworn to return to Ireland to work there as a priest.

At the time of Oliver's ordination the Cromwellian persecutions were at their height in Ireland and he therefore decided to remain in Rome until the situation improved. He took up residence with the Oratorian Fathers and it was presumably during these years that he obtained his doctorate in theology and canon law. His good friend Fr Scarampi died in 1656. In 1657 Oliver was appointed a lecturer in theology and for the next twelve years he lived very happily as a scholar in Rome, mixing with fellow academics. He brought many happy memories of this period back to Ireland with him. He devoted himself to acts of charity in his spare time, especially to the care of the sick in the nearby hospital of Santo Spirito. In addition to these duties he acted as Roman agent for several Irish bishops.

In 1669 Edmund O'Reilly, Archbishop of Armagh, died in France. He had been in exile for many years and the Viceroy had refused him permission to return to Ireland to die. Pope Clement IX decided to appoint Oliver his successor to the See of Armagh. Despite some opposition to this appointment, Oliver was consecrated in Flanders and he then set off on the difficult journey across Europe back to Ireland. He travelled through the Brenner Pass to Innsbruck, then on to Munich, through Augsburg, Nürnberg, and Würzburg to Mainz, then down the Rhine to Cologne. He left Ghent on 3 December 1669 and on 16 December he arrived in London where he was given an audience by the Queen, Catherine of Braganza. Archbishop Plunkett spent almost three months of this bitter winter in London where 'the cold is so intense that the wine of Spain was frozen in my chalice, a heavy fall of snow succeeded the frost so that it is impossible to travel while this cold lasts'.

Oliver finally sailed into Ringsend on the morning of Monday, 10 March 1670. Ireland was still suffering from the ravages of the Cromwellian persecutions. Many priests had been killed, many had fled into exile. Churches and monasteries had been destroyed. The Archbishop threw himself into the task of the reorganisation of the Irish Church. He took up residence not far from Dundalk where the Baron of Louth had offered him hospitality. Shortly afterwards he convened two synods of the diocesan clergy. He also held two ordination ceremonies, and within six weeks he had confirmed more than ten thousand people. However, he estimated that due to the lack of resident bishops during the previous decades there were still at least fifty thousand people throughout Ulster waiting to be confirmed. At the end of that spring he sent a full report to Rome on the affairs of the diocese of Armagh. The Archbishop's next task was to organise schools with the double purpose of training his priests and educating young Catholics. After an existence of only three years and five months, these schools were destroyed in November 1673 during the first outbreak of severe persecution when the Archbishop had to go into hiding. He was so saddened by this occurrence that he later wrote that 'there is nothing that occasions me more inward grief than to see the schools instituted by me now destroyed after so many toils'.

Having set up the schools, the Archbishop then set about reforming the clergy so that they should be trained in ecclesiastical discipline. As he was anxious that the benefit of a Roman training should be made available to a number of his priests, he kept in touch with the affairs of the Irish colleges on the Continent and requested the cardinals of Spain, Portugal, France and Belgium to ensure that students from all parts of Ireland wuld be admitted to the Irish colleges in their countries. Oliver had been in Ireland for only three months when he organised the first Conference of Irish Bishops in Dublin. His

51

St Oliver Plunkett visiting a village in his diocese

chief purpose in doing this was to draw up plans for the
appointment of more bishops and to select a panel of priests
suitable for promotion and forward their names to Rome. He
later held his first Provincial Council at Clones in August 1670.
Under one of the decrees of this Council, priests were forbidden
to frequent taverns and market places and they were instructed

to have a fixed lodging and a fixed place or places for saying Mass. All-night wakes were prohibited and only close relatives and friends of the deceased were to be admitted to his wake. Drinking at wakes was also banned. Diocesan synods of his own Armagh clergy were held frequently during the 1670s.

The Archbishop had to deal with many unpleasant disagreements between some of the Irish clergy, the Dominicans and Franciscans in particular, who were dissatisfied with their role in the Irish Church. This, together with the uncertain political situation, must have made life especially difficult for the Oliver. He was also deeply moved by the reduced status and circumstances of the descendants of the old Irish nobility: 'it truly moves one to compassion to see high families of the house of O'Neill, O'Donnell, McGuire, MacMahon, McGuinness, O'Cahan, O'Kelly, O'Ferrall, who were great princes till the time of Elizabeth and King James, in the memory of my father and of many who are yet living, it moves me to compassion I say to see their children without property and without maintenance and without means of education, yet for the faith they suffered joyfully the loss of their property'.

The events that led up to the imprisonment of the Archbishop who was working so hard to improve the conditions of his people were both complicated and sinister. On 21 October 1679 an instruction was issued to arrest the Archbishop and Bishop Tyrell of Clogher on a charge of plotting to bring a French army to Ireland. Oliver was arrested in Dublin on 6 December and placed in close confinement in a cell in Dublin Castle where he was kept for six weeks. No friends were allowed to visit him until January 1680, nor was he allowed to write letters before then. Even in prison he had financial worries, as he had to provide his own food and clothing, and the damp cells in which he and his servant were confined cost him £1 a week. His friends and relatives willingly helped him out but he found it humiliating to be such a burden to others.

He had been in Dublin Castle for three months before anyone came forward to provide evidence against him. By this time the Viceroy had been informed that an Irish Popish plot had been discovered and that an inquiry was being made into 'treasonable

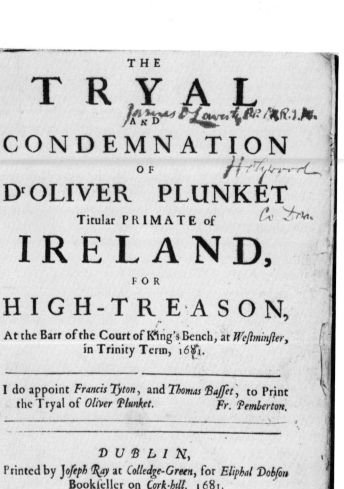

THE

TRYAL
AND

CONDEMNATION

OF

Dr OLIVER PLUNKET

Titular PRIMATE of

IRELAND,

FOR

HIGH-TREASON,

At the Barr of the Court of King's Bench, at *Westminster*, in Trinity Term, 1681.

I do appoint *Francis Tyton*, and *Thomas Basset*, to Print the Tryal of *Oliver Plunket*.   *Fr. Pemberton.*

DUBLIN,

Printed by *Joseph Ray* at *Colledge-Green*, for *Eliphal Dobson* Bookseller on *Cork-hill.* 1681.

Title page of the transcript of the trial of Oliver Plunkett, published 1681

practices in Ireland'. Informers against the Archbishop soon came forward, among them a number of priests who had been disciplined by Oliver on account of the waywardness of their lives, including Fr James Callaghan, Fr Daniel Finnan and Friar

54

John Moyer. As the alleged treasonable acts were supposed to have taken place near Carlingford, County Louth, Viceroy Ormond decided that the trial must take place at Dundalk. It was felt that this arrangement would be to the Archbishop's advantage, as he would then be among his own people and would have little difficulty in gathering witnesses. He was well-known in the locality and friendly with the Protestants of the area, and a local jury could be relied on to treat him with justice. However, because the verdict would be a foregone conclusion under these circumstances, Oliver's opponents fought hard to have the venue changed to Dublin. His friends were not idle during those summer months of 1680. Priests, friars and laymen were willing to come forward to testify on his behalf, and there was little doubt that that verdict would be in his favour.

On 21 July the Privy Council ordered that Oliver be brought to trial at the King's Bench Bar in Dublin, but even as that letter was being written in London, final arrangements had been made and Oliver was being taken to Dundalk under guard. On 23 July he was put on trial before Baron Hartstong and Justice Cusack. As he listened to the bill of indictment he realised that much of it was founded on Moyer's accusations. The trial soon broke down when the Crown witnesses failed to appear. Afterwards, Oliver was brought back to his cell in Dublin Castle, still in ignorance of the charges against him. Counsel was not allowed plead his cause and his witnesses were not sworn. Strangest of all, it was agreed that he would have to be acquitted at three criminal sessions before he would be set free. After the trial in Dundalk it was quite clear that no group of Irishmen, Catholic or Protestant, would condemn Oliver, and for this reason his enemies urged that he be brought to London. Ormond strenuously opposed this move, but despite his intervention, Oliver was ordered to present himself before the Privy Council in London on 6 October. He arrived at Newgate Jail on 29 October and was placed in solitary confinement. Again he had to pay for his room, food, candles , and for charcoal if he wanted a fire. He even had to pay for the shackles on his legs, as all the prisoners wore irons and the lightest in weight were the most expensive. Newgate was indeed a gruesome chamber of horrors. It was unbelievably filthy, without sanitation or facilities for either personal washing or laundry. There was little ventilation and the buildings were damp and infested with vermin. Although the Archbishop was only fifty-eight years old his health was already poor and he was suffering from a number of severe ailments.

On 4 November Oliver was examined before a sub-committee of the Privy Council. No further witnesses against him appear to have been available at that time and he was sent back to his cell. Later in the month Moyer and some of his friends returned to London from Ireland and the north of Ireland was searched for more suitable witnesses. Finally, at least twenty Ulstermen were brought to London in an effort to condemn the Archbishop. Among them were priests and laymen, including four secular priests of Armagh, two secular priests of Clogher and four Franciscans. Not all of this number eventually gave evidence. On 10 November 1680 Oliver appeared before the Bar of the House of Lords and denied that he had had any correspondence with France. When he was asked if he knew of any conspiracies against the English, he expressed his doubts as to their existence, and stated that his own life had been threatened on about a hundred occasions. On 12 February 1681 the bill of indictment against him was presented to the Grand Jury of Westminister, but the witnesses contradicted themselves so blatantly that the Jury rejected the bill. It was not until March that the Grand Jury finally found a true bill against the Archbishop and returned him for trial on a charge of high treason. By that time a petition had been presented to the King requesting that the Archbishop's solitary confinement be alleviated for the sake of his health. The King and the Privy Council decided that he should be given as much liberty within the prison as the Government would allow and that he would be allowed to receive visitors within the hearing of the Governor or his representative. In May 1681 Oliver Plunkett was charged with high treason before the King's bench. Oliver objected to being tried in England for an offence alleged to have been committed in Ireland, but was overruled by Lord Chief Justice Pemberton. He pleaded not guilty and asked for time to have his witnesses brought from Ireland. The trial was fixed for 8 June, five weeks away. He was then given permission to see his servant, but his request that a priest be allowed to meet him was turned down.

Five weeks was an extremely short length of time in which to gather witnesses from Ireland, but the attempt had to be made. The Archbishop decided to call only eight witnesses, each of whom would cost him £20. His servant, McKenna, and relative, John Plunkett, set out for Ireland to collect the witnesses, but their boat was caught in rough seas and it took them more than two weeks to get to Ireland. However, when the witnesses had been gathered together they refused to travel to England until the King would grant them safe conduct. This did not come through until 6 June, by which time McKenna and Plunkett had arrived back in London alone. Oliver appealed to the Court for extra days to allow his witnesses to arrive, but his petition was turned down.

On 8 June Archbishop Plunkett stood without witnesses before his enemies in Westminister Hall. He knew he could expect little sympathy from the judge, jury, his accusers or the audience. After a trial that has since been condmened as a great miscarriage of justice, the Archbishop was found guilty of treason. In his defence, Oliver merely replied that none of the charges against him were true, 'but all plain romance'. On 15 June 1681 the infamous sentence was passed. Before sentencing him, Judge Pemberton, who had conducted the trial, made a strong attack on the Catholic religion and then pronounced the sentence — 'and therefore you must go from thence to the place from which you came, that is to Newgate, and from hence you shall be drawn through the city of London to Tyburn. There you shall be hanged from the neck, cut down before you are dead, your bowels shall be taken out and burned before your face, your head shall be cut off and your body divided in four quarters, to be disposed of as His Majesty please, and I pray to God to have mercy on your soul'.

Oliver's calm courage during the last two weeks as he awaited his execution amazed even himself. He wrote about it to his former secretary, Fr Michael Plunkett, in Rome: 'Sentence of death was passed against me on the 15th without causing me any fear or depriving me of sleep for a quarter of an hour.... I die most willingly, and being the first among the Irish I will teach others with the Grace of God by example not to fear death. I have considered that Christ, by his fears and passion merited for me to be without fear'.

During his last few weeks on earth one of Oliver's fellow prisoners was Dom Maurus Corker, a Yorkshire convert to Catholicism who had become a Benedictine in the Abbey of Lamspringe in Germany. He had been arrested on his return to England and was also accused of involvement in the Popish plot. He was aware of the Archbishop's presence while he was still in solitary confinement, but after Oliver's sentence was pronounced he was allowed to send messages to him and during those last few weeks a correspondence developed between them which is among the most inspiring examples of prison literature. In Oliver's last letter, written on the day before before his execution, he wrote to Dom Corker: 'Sir, I do most earnestly recommend myself to your prayers and to the most holy sacrifices of all the noble confessors who are in the prison and to such priests as you are acquainted with, and I hope soon to be able to requite all your and their kindness. I do recommend to you and to them my most faithful servant James McKenna who served me these eleven years. I desire that you will be pleased to tell all my benefactors that for all eternity I will be mindful of them and that I will pray for them until they will come where I hope to come soon and then will also thank them in the sight of the Supreme Lord. Your obliged friend, Oliver Plunkett'.

Dom Corker preserved reminiscences of the Archbishop's last days in prison, such as: 'The very night before he died, being as it were at heart's ease he went to bed at eleven of the clock and slept quietly and soundly until four in the morning at which time his man who lay in the room with him awaked him. So little concern had he upon his spirit or rather had the loveliness of the end beautified the horror of the passage to it'.

Tyburn was about two miles from Newgate and Oliver was brought over roughly cobbled streets and through growing throngs of people for a journey which must have taken the best part of an hour. The gallows had been erected at what is now the centre of the street at Hyde Park corner. The Archbishop's last speech before his execution was printed in London and translated into several languages including Irish and Italian. In this speech Oliver referred to the short time which had been allowed to him to bring witnesses and documents from Ireland to help in his defence and he once again denied the accusations which were made against him at the trial. He declared that he had performed the functions of a Catholic bishop as long as he was permitted to do so, and had tried by preaching and by making regulations to reform the clergy. He then forgave the priests who had sworn falsely against him as well as all those who had played a part in his death.

After the terrible execution, some friends of the Archbishop obtained possession of his remains and kept them until Dom Corker was released from prison in 1683. He then had the body exhumed and removed most of the relics to the Benedictine monastery of Lamspringe in Germany. Shortly afterwards he brought the martyr's head to Rome and deposited it in the care of Cardinal Howard. It was kept in Rome until about 1720 when it was given to the Archbishop of Armagh. He brought it to the Dominican nuns in Drogheda about thirteen years later. Mother Catherine Plunkett, a relative of the martyr, was Prioress of this convent, and the precious relic remained there for nearly two centuries until 29 June 1921 when it was transferred to St Peter's Church in Drogheda, where it may still be seen.

The rest of Oliver's body remained in a special shrine in Lamspringe for about two centuries, and in 1883 when this Abbey was secularised the relics were transferred to Downside Abbey in England. In 1975 portions of these relics were brought from Downside to Ireland. Many other relics found their way to several parts of Europe and even to the United States. One of the more important of these is a rib bone which is now in the Siena Convent in Drogheda. Mass vestments belonging to the Archbishop are now in the custody of the Bishop of Meath, and his episcopal ring is in the possession of his cousin, Lord Dunsany. A chalice and thurible belonging to him are in Clonliffe College in Dublin and a portion of another thurible is in the Maynooth College museum.

Although Oliver Plunket was given the title 'martyr'

immediately after his execution, for various reasons no effort was made to have his cause examined by Rome. This may have been due partly to the Penal Laws which remained in force in Ireland for another century. He remained almost forgotten until the second half of the nineteenth century when some research into his life was undertaken. After that, a number of both popular and scholarly studies were published, and on Whit Sunday 1920, in the presence of Cardinal Logue, Oliver's fifteenth successor in Armagh, and a great crowd of cardinals, bishops and priests and about fifty thousand lay people, Oliver was solemnly beatified in St Peter's Basilica in Rome.

During the following years there was a great effort made to spread the story of Oliver's life and to attract pilgrims to his shrine in Drogheda. Petitions for his canonisation were sent to Rome by the Irish hierarchy in 1935 but the big breakthrough did not come until 1958 when a dying woman, Signora Giovanna Martiriggiano, regained consciousness and showed signs of recovery after prayers had been said to Blessed Oliver for her cure. Monsignor John Hanley was appointed postulator in 1969 having already secured his doctorate in Rome for a thesis on Blessed Oliver's pastoral work. It was eventually announced that Oliver would be canonised in St Peter's in Rome on Sunday, 12 October 1975.

Dozens of articles about St Oliver were published in newspapers, religious magazines and historical periodicals, and a twenty-five minute documentary film was made by the Radharc group for RTE television. This film was scripted by Fr Desmond Forristal, author of the play *The True Story of the Horrid Popish Plot*.

Loughcrew in County Meath, the birthplace of Oliver Plunkett is now a place of pilgrimage. Many people will be familiar with the yew-walk leading from the church to the Norman motte and the remains of an old mill. The walk is said to be one of the finest in Ireland and, according to tradition, was planted by the Plunketts. North Louth also contains many landmarks associated with Oliver's decade as Archbishop of Armagh, among them the tiny churches of Ballybarrack just south of Dundalk, and Ardpatrick, which is situated on a hill overlooking the village of Louth.

St Oliver Plunkett is the fourth saint to have been canonised since the introduction of Christianity to Ireland. Patrick and Columbanus have always been recognised as belonging to the universal Calendar of Saints. The other three saints to have been formally canonised are St Fergal or Virgilius of Salzburg, St Malachy Ó Morgair and St Laurence O'Toole.

6

YPRES TO KYLEMORE — THE STORY OF THE IRISH BENEDICTINE NUNS

> She said, "They gave me of their best,
> Their lives, they gave their lives for me;
> I tossed them to the howling waste
> And flung them to the foaming sea".
>
> She said, "I never gave them aught,
> Not mine the power, if mine the will;
> I let them starve, I let them bleed -
> They bled and starved, and loved me still".
>
> *Emily Lawless*

This poem, 'After Aughrim' refers to the fate of the Wild Geese, those noblemen and militants who left Ireland after the Treaty of Limerick in 1691 to fight as mercenaries in continental Europe. The lives and fates of a small group of Irish Benedictine nuns, many of them aristocrats, were tied up with the fate of the Wild Geese and the vain hope of the restoration of a Stuart king to the English throne.

After the defeat of the combined Irish and French armies at Aughrim, about twenty thousand men, including Patrick Sarsfield, sailed to Brest in Brittany to form the bulk of the famous Irish Brigade in the Netherlands. They were merely the forerunners of a great exodus of Irishmen who fled from the hardship caused by the Penal Laws to fight for France, Spain and Austria. It is said that 150,000 Irishmen died in the service of France between 1691 and 1745. These Wild Geese were thus named by the romantic and sorrowful Irish people, and they had the careless courage and lived the wild life of men who had nothing to lose — 'war-battered dogs' — as Emily Lawless referred to them in another poem. The bitterness was matched only by their longing to return to their native country, but they were prevented from doing this by the regular enactment of new laws against Catholics in Ireland.

The Irish Benedictine nuns had their convent at Ypres in Belgium. Abbeys had been founded in Belgium since the reign of King Henry VIII when monasteries and religious houses throughout England, among them three hundred Benedictine Abbeys, were plundered and suppressed. From that time onwards, many young English and Irish people sought refuge on the Continent to enjoy the freedom of conscience which was denied them at home.

Lady Mary Percy, whose father, Thomas, Earl of Northumberland was martyred during the reign of Queen Elizabeth I, was among the English noblewomen who founded a Benedictine Abbey for English exiles in Brussels. Its numbers increased rapidly, and another house was established in Ghent, followed by a third at Ypres. The Ypres Abbey was then handed over to the Irish nuns who were known in Flanders as 'Der Iersche Damen' — the Irish Dames. This Irish Abbey endured for some two hundred and fifty years through wars that shook the very pillars of Europe.

In the first years after its foundation the existence of the Abbey at Ypres was precarious and it only managed to keep going with the help of additional novices from Ireland. In 1686 the first Irish Abbess was elected. She was Dame Mary Butler of the ancient and noble family of the Butlers of Kilkenny, a cousin of the Duke of Ormond, who was one of the most influential personalities in the Irish and English political circles of his day.

Abbess Butler had been in office only a short time when she was invited by the Stuart King James II to play a prominent part in establishing a house of Benedictine nuns in Dublin. The King had known the nuns when he was in exile in the Low Countries, and had held them in high esteem. In fact, the Stuarts, and King Charles II especially, had been greatly indebted to the Order of St Benedict for years, and it was largely due to a member of the Order that the Merry Monarch escaped after the disastrous

Courtyard of the Benedictine Abbey at Ypres

Battle of Worcester in 1651. A manuscript which was preserved in the Abbey of Ypres gave the following account of the Dublin foundation: 'Anno i.e. in the year 1687, King James the Second, desirous of establishing a convent of religious women in Ireland, ordered the Duke of Tyrconnel, his Lord Lieutenant in said Kingdom, to write to the Lady Abbess of the Irish Dames of Ypres, and desire she would repair to Dublin, and establish her monastery in that city'. The manuscript describes Abbess Butler as 'the person most proper for that effect; begging that the Vicars General would reserve the house of Ypres for a place of refuge in case of an adverse change in the times'. Under the King's orders a house for the nuns was taken in Little Ship Street at the back of Dublin Castle.

On her way to Dublin Abbess Butler travelled through London and met the Queen in Whitehall 'in the great habit of her order' which had not been seen there since the time of the religious persecutions. When she arrived in Dublin she was presented to the King and he ordered a royal patent to be granted to the Benedictines 'with the most ample privileges, as his first chief and royal Abbey'. This royal patent was dated 5 June 1689.

On 1 July 1690, King James' army was defeated by King William of Orange at the Battle of the Boyne. The victorious army marched into Dublin and ransacked the new monastery. Abbess Butler sent her postulants back to their parents' homes for safety, and she and some of her nuns managed to save a quantity of the church plate and ornaments. She then decided to return to Ypres, and her cousin the Duke of Ormond obtained a safe pass for her and her community to leave the country.

By this time King James had been finally defeated and he fled to France. With him went the hopes of the Irish and he was followed by the Wild Geese who held themselves bound in honour to James and who hoped one day to return to Ireland with him. Referring to the departure of the first Wild Geese the historian Edmund Curtis said: 'Seldom in history have a few thousand men, departing into exile, represented as these did almost the whole aristocracy, the fighting force, and the hope of a nation'.

After the violent break-up of her community, and while these momentous events were taking place in Ireland, Abbess Butler returned to Ypres. During this time of bitter trial many benefactors contributed towards the upkeep of the community. Pope Innocent XIII forwarded a sum of one thousand scudi, which was part of a larger sum set aside by him for the relief of distressed Irish exiles. The King of France allowed the nuns an annual sum of five hundred florins, while Queen Mary of Modena, wife of James II, also made contributions to 'the daughters of such as followed her husband's fortunes'. The Abbess gradually gathered together a small number of novices for her convent, and was still building up the community when she died in 1723 after sixty-six years of religious profession and thirty-eight years as Abbess.

Abbess Butler's long term of office witnessed the beginning and the end of the War of the Spanish Succession which broke out in 1704 and ended with the Peace of Utrecht in 1713. This war must have been a source of unusual interest and anxiety for the Irish Dames of Ypres, not only because many of the decisive battles were fought in Belgium, known for so long as 'the cockpit of Europe', but also because the nuns had friends and relatives in the Irish Brigade — the Wild Geese who had scorned to join the victorious King William in Ireland because they regarded him as a usurper. Abbess Butler's cousin, the Duke of Ormond, was one of those who fought in the war. The Battle of Oudenarde in east Flanders, in which Fitzgerald's and O'Brien's Irish Regiments of Foot and Nugent's Regiment of Horse fought on the French side, was fought out within a day's journey of Ypres. At this battle the Irish Brigade created a new standard for the French army, and five Irish colonels were afterwards decorated with the Grand Cross of the Order of St Louis.

In 1706 the memorable Battle of Ramillies, in which the Irish Regiment played a prominent part, was fought. Its commander was Lord Clare, a kinsman of one of the nuns of Ypres Abbey. After the battle, the flag of Ramillies was captured by the Irish and deposited by them in the Abbey. It now hangs among the treasures in the great hallway of Kylemore Abbey. The victory of Ramillies saved the French Army from total disaster, and the marching song that celebrated it resounded through Europe:

> The flags we conquered in that fray
> Look lone in Ypres Choir, they say.
> We'll win them company today —
> Or bravely die like Clare's Dragoons.

The flags of victory were brought to the Abbey by Murrough O'Brien, a cousin of Lord Clare. Only a portion of one of the original three has survived. It is dark blue in colour with a large Harp of Erin in reddish gold. It was hidden in the cellars of Ypres

Portion of the Flag of Ramillies now preserved in the Benedictine Abbey, Kylemore

Abbey during the first world war. Lord Clare was wounded nine times during the Battle of Ramillies and he died a few days later at Brussels, at the age of thirty-six. He was buried with many other Irish exiles in the Church of the Holy Cross, Louvain. There was a huge death-toll at the battle, and many other officers were killed.

There is another poignant association between the Battle of Ramillies and Ypres Abbey. There is a tale of a heart-broken girl whose lover was killed in the fighting and who came to the Abbey to pray for the repose of his soul. Her name has not been recorded but it is said that she remained at the Abbey for the rest of her life. Thomas Davis identified her as Eily, 'The Flower of Finae', and the final verse of his poem about her is:

> In the cloisters of Ypres a banner is swaying
> And by it a pale, weeping maiden is praying;
> That flag's the sole trophy of Ramillies fray
> This nun is poor Eily, the Flower of Finae.

As the years went by the Irish Brigade was drafted to other fronts in England, Germany and Austria as they were needed. The war of the Austrian succession revived the conflict in Belgium. At the battle of Fontenoy the English and Hanoverian ranks were broken by the cavalry charge of men whose war cry was 'remember Limerick'. The Commander here was Charles O'Brien, sixth Earl of Clare, the son of the hero of Ramillies. He followed up his victory at Rocoux and Leffelt, and also defended Malines. Like his distinguished father, he was made a Marshal of France. George II of England, who witnessed some of these battles, exclaimed bitterly: 'Cursed be the laws that deprive me of such gallant soldiers'.

While these battles were raging around Ypres, life in the Benedictine cloister continued as normally as possible under the circumstances. The nuns lived active and contemplative lives according to the rule of the Order. New postulants continued to come from Ireland, even though sometimes in very small numbers. The nuns established schools and gave charitable assistance to the poor of the area. Because of the unique location of their Abbey they were known to many of the ruling families of Europe and received correspondence and gifts from many royal houses. It is said that the teaching of the nuns served as a bulwark against Lutheran and Calvinist free thinking in the seventeeth century.

Among the treasures of the Abbey were several precious relics given by King James II, or sent from Rome by James III and his son the Cardinal Duke of York. It must be remembered that the nuns of Ypres remained staunch supporters of the Stuart cause until the last flicker of hope of restoration died with Bonnie Prince Charlie. One of the other treasures was a piece of lace worked by Mary Queen of Scots and her maids of honour, and presented to the nuns by James II. There were also portraits of several Abbesses and one of James II.

The convent archives contained a considerable collection of letters written by the various abbesses to the heads of the exiled Stuarts, together with the replies to many of these letters. There were thirty-seven letters in all, beginning at the end of the seventeenth century with those from Abbess Butler to Queen Mary of Modena and extending as far as 1766, the year of the death of James III. The Stuart cause received its death-blow when Prince Charles and his Highlanders were defeated at the Battle of Culloden in 1746. Charles' younger brother Henry had visited the convent at Ypres and soon afterwards decided to give up his claim to the throne and become a priest. He later became a Cardinal and was known as the Cardinal Duke of York. For many years after the Battle of Culloden, while Charles wandered around the Continent, the nuns continued to correspond with him and to send him gifts.

A new epoch in the history of the Irish Dames of Ypres began when the French Revolution broke out. The nuns were expelled, but a great storm broke out which prevented their boat from sailing and the *Commissaires* were unable to carry out the edict on time. In that critical interval Robespierre fell, and the whole situation was altered.

When the Abbess Bernard Lynch was elected in 1799 the persecuting regime of the Revolution was still at its height. A few months later Napoleon began his career as First Consul and Emperor. At the beginning of his regime religious persecution ceased, but an order for the suppression of the community was soon issued. Through the offices of General Dillon and General James O'Moran the Abbess was given an audience with Napoleon to plead for the safety of her nuns. Napoleon told her that he had 'the deepest respect for your nation', and while his troops patrolled Ypres and the Grand Army marched through Flanders on the way to Moscow, the Irish Abbey remained safe. However, there were other difficulties, for in the spring of 1810 three nuns died of fever, reducing the community to only fourteen members.

By this time the glories of the Irish Brigade were coming to an end. The many battles they had fought had been of no avail in serving the Irish cause and the great families were now scattered.

During the century after the Battle of Waterloo there was a lull in international conflict, but there was still internal political strife in the Low Countries which culminated in the withdrawal of Belgium from Dutch rule. The nuns used this period to expand their work of education and to embark on a building programme. Instead of the quaint old monastic building that had served them so well while armies massed themeselves around the walls of Ypres, the nuns erected a new Abbey. It was a fine example of the Flemish Gothic style built in red brick with that essential feature of monastic architecture, square cloisters. The chapel in the Abbey was a centre of great devotion for the townspeople, and the Abbey itself became renowned for its care of the poor of the area, for whom the nuns prepared a meal each day.

This comparatively normal life was disrupted by the outbreak of the first world war. The ramparts of Ypres were bombarded by German shells, and the whole town was bombed. Meanwhile, the plight of the wounded soldiers and civilians was well-known in Ireland, and groups were set up to send them first aid material and supplies. Among those who sent aid were the people of Moate, County Westmeath, and a painting hanging in the Convent of Mercy there was sent from Ypres as a token of gratitude. It depicts Christ walking among the wounded soldiers in the bombed Cathedral of Ypres.

One of the Irish Benedictines, Dame M. Columban, wrote the story of the events leading up to the bombing of Ypres and the evacuation of the Royal Abbey in *The Irish Nuns at Ypres: an episode of the war* (ed. R.Barry O'Brien, introduction by John Redmond MP). This gave a detailed account of all that happened to the community from the arrival of the Germans at

Ypres to the safe arrival of the nuns at Oulton Abbey.

On 31 July 1914 the British Government demanded an undertaking from the French and German governments to respect Belgium's neutrality in accordance with treaty obligations, and demanded from the Belgian government an undertaking to uphold it. Germany did not respond to this demand, and from that time war was inevitable. On 3 August Belgium was invaded by German troops and Liège was attacked. Many other Belgian towns were destroyed and the battle of Ypres began in earnest on 11 October. The town, defended by the Allies, held out heroically, but Ypres became the centre of what was probably the most terrible fighting of the war.

The news of the German invasion was brought to the cloistered Benedictines by some poor people who came to the Abbey every day to receive soup. Even at that early stage one poor woman offered her little house as a shelter for the Abbess, who had been paralysed by a stroke two years previously. Food became increasingly scarce as the armies overran the town, and life became chaotic due to the intermittent gunfire and the scream of German planes dropping bombs over the besieged city. It was decided that each nun should prepare an emergency parcel of necessities in case they had to flee from the Abbey.

Soon hundreds of refugees from the towns and villages in the firing line crowded into the streets of Ypres, even though the town was already full of soldiers. Dinner and supper were distributed to the refugees each day at the Abbey doors. When a law was issued ordering the expulsion of all Germans resident in Belgium, four German sisters were forced to leave the community. These first victims of the war, all of whom had spent over twenty-five years in the enclosed convent, were evacuated to Holland.

The paralysed Abbess clearly could not leave in a hurry, and she was sent to a safe place outside Ypres. Meanwhile, the nuns brought bedding and provisions to the cellar for safety and they were also advised to pile up sand and earth against the cellar windows to deaden the force of the shells should they come in their direction. The precious treasures, archives and antiquities of the Abbey had already been placed in security.

71

It is believed that at one stage the Germans had a million men in the neighbourhood, and both Allies and Germans sustained frightful losses. Ambulances continually brought in wounded victims from the battlefields. The classrooms, children's dormitory, library, noviceship and workroom were prepared as a makeshift hospital for the wounded, but before they could be used another more suitable place was found. The nuns spent all their free time rolling bandages for the wounded. The tabernacle was emptied in case of desecration, and the sanctuary lamp was extinguished. As the war escalated many of the inhabitants of Ypres abandoned their houses and property and left the town, anxious only to save their lives. The fighting continued in the air, and on all sides. Refugees crowded into the Abbey.

Eventually, everybody appeared to have deserted the stricken town, and the Benedictines feared for their own safety and for that of their Abbey. The Mother Prioress and two of the sisters decided to seek information at the British Headquarters — the sisters who had been cloistered for so long now had to make their way on foot past rubble and debris through a town which they hardly recognised. They went to several influential people, friends of the Abbey, only to find that their premises were locked up, and that they had left the town. Eventually it was decided that the nuns would take refuge at Poperinghe, about ten miles from Ypres, in the hope that they would be able to get from there to England. The nuns departed sadly from their Abbey, pushing their possessions in a handcart. The town was in a dreadful state as they left. There were clouds of smoke everywhere from bursting shells and falling buildings, and after a weary journey the group arrived at Poperinghe.

There was now a further period of waiting and indecision before the Benedictines knew what their fate was to be. They used this time to visit the wounded soldiers. They also made heroic attempts to revisit their Abbey at Ypres. However, they soon realised that they must abandon all hope of returning there. Plans had already been made to have the community evacuated to England where they were given a hospitable reception at the Benedictine Abbey of Oulton in Staffordshire. The British military authorities provided ambulances and sea passage for the nuns to Dover.

After spending some time at Oulton Abbey the Benedictine writer and abbot, Dom Columba Marmion,became interested in the welfare of the Irish Benedictines. The nuns then found a temporary home at Macmine Castle, County Wexford. Their fortunes took another dramatic turn when it was decided that they would settle at Kylemore Castle, in the north-west of Connemara, County Galway. They were welcomed by the Archbishop of Tuam, Most Rev. Dr Gilmartin, and all the rights and privileges of Ypres Abbey were transferred to Kylemore by the Holy See.

The Bishop of Bruges, to whose diocese Ypres belonged, heard of the decision with regret. 'This Irish Abbey,' he said 'was one of the glories of our Flanders.'

However, by this time the Irish Benedictines had financial problems. Although the Belgian assets of the community should have covered the cost of the Kylemore property, devaluation and inflation problems, together with the refusal of the British government to allow war reparations for the ruined Abbey cut off all hope of finance from these sources. Two members of the community went to London where, under the auspices of T.P. O'Connor, journalist and statesman, Sir John Lavery, the artist, and other influential people, they made a public appeal for funds. At the same time the community set about organising a secondary school at Kylemore Abbey.

The new home of the Benedictines had a fascinating if somewhat tragic history. The castle itself was built to fulfil the honeymoon wish of the young wife of a wealthy London surgeon and financier, Mitchell Henry. During their honeymoon, the couple travelled from Galway through the wild beauty of Connemara, and stopped for a picnic on the roadside near Kylemore Pass. While much of the beauty of Connemara is barren and rugged, there is more of a fairytale quality around Kylemore which resembles areas of the Austrian Alps with its wooded slopes reflected in the lake and the full circle of the granite mountain chain forming a great backdrop. Kylemore Abbey today, with its white granite facade reflected in the deep calm waters of the lake, is one of the best known and loved scenes of Irish beauty which regularly appears in our tourist literature and picture postcards. However, when Mrs Mitchell Henry first saw Kylemore, there was just one solitary dwelling, a shooting lodge on the hill behind the lake.

When the couple returned to London, Mr Henry started negotiations for the purchase of the shooting lodge and nine thousand acres of mountain, lake and moor from the owners, the Blakes. When the deal was completed the Henrys started to plan the layout of the property as their ancestral home. Kylemore Castle was designed by two architects of considerable ability and sensitivity — Usher Roberts and John F. Fuller.

The harmony and elegance of the interior of the Castle combined with the majestic setting to create an atmosphere of great beauty. Everywhere there is evidence of superb craftmanship — handtooled limestone on the exterior, patterned marquetry in the Great Hall, hand-carved marble and onyx fireplaces, richly ornamented Italian ceilings, oak wall panelling, lead light windows and ornate gilded pelmets. The Hall was embellished with triple arches of cut stone upon pillars of Connemara marble.

There were seventy rooms in the Castle and the workmanship and materials throughout were of the highest standard. The labour was local, but Italian experts were called in for the ceilings and other specialised work. The Gothic church in the grounds was in harmony with the Castle. It is a replica of Norwich Cathedral which was originally built by the English Benedictines.

Great care was also taken with the exterior layout of the Castle. The avenue was a mile long, and was bordered by trees and shrubs from many parts of the world. At the west side was the Italian garden, and there were fruit and vegetable gardens covering an area of eight acres. In the model farm building there were byres and stables, kennels and poultry houses. Drinking water was provided from the natural springs of Mweelin mountain, and the Castle had its own lighting plant.

The Castle took seven years to build, and it is estimated that the project cost Mitchell Henry £1,250,000 — an immense sum at that time.

Mitchell Henry and his wife had nine children. At Kylemore

Castle they were hosts of distinction and culture, and many famous personalities in the world of politics, high finance, art and literature were entertained there.

The Henrys had lived at Kylemore Castle for seven years when Mrs Henry went on a trip to Egypt. There she developed 'Nile Fever' and after a few days illness, died in Cairo. Her husband arranged to have her body brought back to the mausoleum in Kylemore. After this he lived mainly in London, and in 1902 the Castle and the estate were sold for about a twentieth of the outlay of its construction. In 1903 King Edward VII and Queen Alexandra visited the Castle briefly. It eventually ended up in the hands of caretakers, and the estate and buildings were badly neglected. It was in this condition when the Irish Benedictine nuns arrived from war-battered Ypres to the peaceful and beautiful Connemara setting.

Here the community of about thirty nuns set about restoring order to their lives. The boarding school which was started in

Kylemore Abbey, Co. Galway

75

Ypres in the eighteenth century re-opened, and now there are about a hundred boarders and seventy day girls in Kylemore. The last nun to be professed in Ypres died in 1972, thus severing the final living connection with the Belgian Abbey. A large modern school now stands on the site of the Royal Irish Abbey.

Happily, many memtoes from Ypres have been preserved in Kylemore — they include vestments, chalices, ciboria, monstrances, a thurible, a tabernacle, pewter plates, pictures, statues and, of course, the famous flag of Ramillies. Unfortunately, there were two great fires in Kylemore Abbey in which many of the precious archives and letters brought from Ypres were destroyed.

The Abbey is one of Connemara's major tourist attractions. Approximately twenty thousand tourists sign the visitor's book each year, and probably as many more just pay a visit to the Abbey. In recent years a pottery has been set up, and Connemara flora such as fuschia and mosses are used to decorate the beautifully-turned vases and cruets which are made there. There are also a craft shop and tea-rooms.

And all the while the torrents tumble down the wooded precipice at the back of the Abbey, while the Abbey itself is reflected in the still water of the sheltered lake. Among the mementoes from the days of glory in Ypres there is a portrait of Margaret Vaughan, Mrs Mitchell Henry, whose romantic vision and impeccable good taste caused natural and man-made beauty to combine so beautifully in Kylemore Abbey.

Bibliography

ANDERSON, A.O. *and* M.O. (eds.)., *Adomnan's Life of Columba* (London: Nelson, 1961)

BIELER, Ludwig, *Ireland, Harbinger of the Middle Ages* (London: Oxford University Press, 1963)

CONCANNON, Mrs Thomas, *The Life of St Columban* (Dublin: Catholic Truth Society, 1915)

de PAOR, Máire *and* Liam, *Early Christian Ireland* (London: Thames & Hudson, 1958)

GOUGAUD, Dom Louis. *Christianity in the Celtic Lands* (London: Sheed and Ward, 1932)

KENNY, James F. *Sources for the Early History of Ireland* (New York, Columbia University Press, 1929)

LEHANE, Brendan, *The Quest of Three Abbots* (London: Murray, 1968)

LITTLE, Dr George A., *Brendan the Navigator* (Dublin, Gill, 1945)

NOLAN, Dom Patrick, *The Irish Dames of Ypres* (Dublin, Brown & Nolan, 1908)

O'BOYLE, Very Rev. James Canon, *Life of St Malachy* (Belfast: Quinn, 1931)

Ó FIAICH, (Cardinal) Tomás, *Columbanus in his own Words* (Dublin: Veritas, 1974)

Ó FIAICH, (Cardinal) Tomás, *Saint Oliver at Armagh* (Dublin: Veritas, 1981)

RYAN, John, *Irish Monasticism* (London: Longmans, 1931)

Saint Oliver Plunkett canonisation commemorative booklet.

SCOTT, A. Brian, *Malachy* (Dublin: Veritas, 1976)

SEVERIN, Tim, *The Brendan Voyage* (London: Hutchinson, 1978)

STOKES, Margaret, *Six Months in The Appenines* (London: Bell, 1892)

STOKES, Margaret, *Three Months in the Forests of France* (London: Bell, 1895)

77